How to . . .

get the most from your
COLES NOTES

Key Point

Basic concepts in point form.

Close Up

Additional hints, notes, tips or background information.

Watch Out!

Areas where problems frequently occur.

Quick Tip

Concise ideas to help you learn what you need to know.

Remember This!

Essential material for mastery of the topic.

How to get an **A** in ...

Economics

Market theory

Money & banking

Exercises & practice

sample exam

© Copyright 2000 and Published by
COLES PUBLISHING. A division of Prospero Books
Toronto – Canada
Printed in Canada

Cataloguing in Publication Data

Simpson, Dave, 1942–
How to get an A in — economics: market theory,
money & banking, exercises and sample exam

(Coles notes)
Written by Dave Simpson.
ISBN 0-7740-0617-X

1. Economics. II. Title. III. Series.

HB171.5.S57 2000   330   C00-931263-3

Publisher: Nigel Berrisford
Editing: Paul Kropp Communications
Book design and layout: Karen Petherick

Manufactured by Webcom Limited
Cover finish: Webcom's Exclusive DURACOAT

Contents

CHAPTER ONE

Laying down the foundation

OPPORTUNITY COST

Economics is often defined as the science of choice in a world of scarce resources. Resources are scarce because people have unlimited wants that are beyond the capacity of an economy. Choice involves comparing the value of one action against the value or real cost of an alternative action.

Let's say Joe must decide between keeping his job at the local fast-food restaurant or playing on the school hockey team. If Joe decides to play hockey and quits his job and someone asks what it will cost, Joe will likely list explicit costs like the cost of his hockey equipment. Economists, however, would emphasis the implicit costs to Joe such as lost wages. Implicit costs, which economists refer to as **real** or **opportunity costs,** are defined as the value of a resource used in its next best use. In Joe's case the opportunity costs of playing hockey include the wages lost by not working at the restaurant.

This fundamental economic concept can be illustrated using a **production possibilities curve**. This curve measures the quantity of two goods that can be produced by an economy with a fixed amount of resources. See Diagram 1.1 for a theoretical example of beer versus robots. Any point on the curve such as point D represents the maximum amount of the two goods that can be produced with full employment of all resources. Schedule 1.1 lists the opportunity costs associated with each change in production.

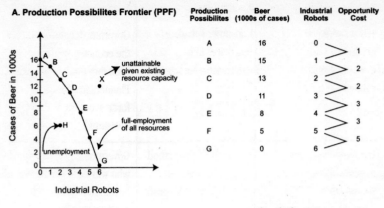

A. Production Possibilites Frontier (PPF)	Production Possibilites	Beer (1000s of cases)	Industrial Robots	Opportunity Cost
	A	16	0	
				1
	B	15	1	
				2
	C	13	2	
				2
	D	11	3	
				3
	E	8	4	
				3
	F	5	5	
				5
	G	0	6	

Diagram 1.1   Schedule 1.1

Let's suppose that an economy operating at point B is producing 15,000 cases of beer and one robot. If the economy moves to position C, it can produce 13,000 cases of beer and two robots. Thus the real cost of producing the second robot is 2,000 cases of beer. The real cost of producing all six robots is 16,000 cases of beer. The real cost of making each additional robot increases, which makes the curve concave to the origin. It is concave because some resources are more productive making beer than they are at making robots. So as the economy moves away from beer towards robot production, the first resources to shift are resources that add little to beer production but add a lot to robot production (for example, electrical engineers). The production possibilities curve is also concave because of the law of diminishing returns at work (which we'll cover in Chapter 4).

ECONOMIC SYSTEMS AND THE FOUR FUNDAMENTAL QUESTIONS

The production possibilities curve illustrates the available combinations of production possibilities for an economy at a fixed point in time. What remains to be determined is **what** combination of production should be selected, **how** the economy should produce the goods, **who** should get to consume the goods and **how much** should be produced. There are basically two methods used to answer these four questions – the **market** and the **command** systems. Here are the differences.

	Market system	**Command system**
What should be produced? For example: beer or robots?	Consumer spending sets prices that determine what firms produce.	Government planners direct the economy to produce what they think is needed. Planners inspire or force acceptance of their decisions.
How will the goods be produced? For example, should labor or capital intensive methods be used?	The production method used is the one that results in the most profit.	Government planners decide who will work where and how to deploy available capital.
Who will get the goods and **how much** will be produced?	Those who can afford the most get the most. Economic inequality, resource depletion and pollution are difficult issues.	In theory distribution is based on need. In practice who you know and being first in line help. Government officials decide who gets how much.
Resource ownership	**Private**	**Government (public)**
Common descriptors	• capitalism • free enterprise • laissez-faire • survival of the fittest • invisible hand • competition • consumer is king • focus on individual rights	• socialism • communism • cradle to grave economic security • from each according to their ability to each according to their need • co-operation • what is good for society as a whole is more important than individual rights

Canada operates as a market system but there are elements of the command system present. For example, governments impose minimum wage laws on the market because governments believe that the market, if left alone, would set unskilled wage rates too low. If a Canadian television station doesn't air enough Canadian content, the government will revoke its broadcasting license. Economic systems operating today, with the exceptions of China, Cuba and North Korea, are market systems with varying amounts of the command system, depending on local conditions.

ECONOMICS AND THE SCIENTIFIC METHOD

Is it possible to construct economic laws that predict human behavior given that each person has a free will to decide how he or she will behave? Scientific observation has shown that while the behavior of a single individual may be difficult to predict, the behavior of groups can be predicted with a good deal of accuracy. For example, if the price of butter falls, consumers will buy more butter. Maybe you, personally, wouldn't purchase butter at any price, but consumers as a group would. Economics is a body of knowledge based on the assumption that human behavior can be predicted.

Like all sciences, economics uses the scientific method to develop theories. The scientific method consists of four basic steps:

1. observations that lead to questions about events
2. collection of data relevant to the events
3. formulation of a possible explanation to the question (an hypothesis)
4. testing the hypothesis to see if it holds up (If it does, the hypothesis becomes an economic theory.)

Economic **concepts** (principles) are generalizations about the nature of something (for example, opportunity costs). An economic **law** is a predictable relationship among two or more variables. For example, the law of demand states that the quantity demanded of a good varies inversely with its price. An economic **theory** is a set of laws that not only predicts but also explains why things happen (for example, theory of price determination). An economic **model** is a set of theories that predicts and explains how the whole economy operates (for example, the Keynesian model of national income determination).

Macroeconomics studies aggregate (total) performance of all markets and large subsections of the economy like government, foreign trade and labor markets.

Microeconomics studies small economic units like individual markets and individual firms. Chapters 2, 3 and 4 deal with micro topics and the rest of the book deals with macro topics.

Ceteris paribus assumption

When conducting an experiment in a chemistry lab, you try to eliminate outside or exogenous variables like temperature changes, enabling you to focus on the particular variables under study. In economics an exogenous change is a change in economic activity resulting from a non-economic cause. Economic experiments can't be controlled in this manner because economic experiments are conducted in the real world where exogenous variables can't be excluded. Therefore, economists make assumptions that state, at the outset, the limitations of an experiment. The **ceteris paribus assumption** states that all other things remain constant. For example, we said previously that if the price of butter falls, consumers will buy more butter. But what if consumers were told that butter was bad for their health, an exogenous change? Butter consumption might fall. This result reduces the credibility of the prediction. So economists say that if the price of butter falls, ceteris paribus, consumers will buy more butter. This doesn't eliminate the problem of faulty economic predictions but it does set the conditions under which the prediction is accurate.

Rational decision-making assumption

Confronted with a choice, economists assume that individuals will weigh alternatives in a rational manner and select the option that will most improve their economic well-being. Again, this may not always be true, but it is a basic economic assumption.

Terminology

Like other subjects economics has its own language. What makes the language of economics difficult is that it takes words in common use and redefines them. For example, to most of us the word "investment" means a purchase of securities like stocks and bonds, but in economics, " investment" means money used to build a capital good like a new factory. As an aid, newly introduced economic terms appear in boldface and are defined in the context of economics.

Positive and normative economics

Normative economics is concerned with the way things ought to be. **Positive economics** describes and analyzes the way things are, without passing judgment. For example, suppose the government wants to implement a policy that will reduce the rate of inflation. Positive economics would analyze the hypothesis that raising the unemployment rate would lower the inflation rate. Normative economics might say that raising the unemployment rate is too high a price to pay for a small reduction in the rate of inflation.

Practice Exercise

1. Match the term to the statement that it is most closely associated with.

   terms: normative economics; microeconomics; capital; hypothesis; ceteris parabus; macroeconomics; rational thinking; positive economics; consumer is king

   (a) Income should be distributed more evenly.
   (b) Other things remain unchanged.
   (c) The study of individual consumer behavior.
   (d) How the market system decides what is produced.
   (e) Part of the process associated with the scientific method.
   (f) Used to produce consumer goods.
   (g) The basic nature of man according to economists.

2. The schedule below represents the production possibilities of an economy that produces two types of goods – consumer goods and capital goods.

Production Possibilities	#1	#2	#3	#4	#5	#6
Capital Goods	0	1	2	3	4	5
Consumer Goods	20	18	15	11	6	0

   With reference to the above schedule what is the opportunity cost in each of the following cases.

   (a) all 5 capital goods _____
   (b) all 20 consumer goods _____
   (c) the first 3 capital goods _____
   (d) the third capital good _____
   (e) the first 11 consumer goods _____

CHAPTER TWO

How the supply and demand market works

The theory of price determination explains how the forces of demand and supply work together to determine prices. The important assumptions relevant to this theory are:

- The ideal market is assumed to be **perfectly competitive**. This means that the market has many buyers and sellers, none of whom can influence the price of the product through their own independent actions. Everyone in the market is a **price-taker**. Each theoretical firm produces an identical product (**homogeneous**). Everyone has complete knowledge about market conditions and there are no artificial barriers keeping anyone out of the market.
- The time frame under consideration is the **short run**. Economists define this as a period of time when some costs of production are fixed (for example, specialized machinery) and some costs are variable (for example, unskilled labor).
- Until further notice all things will remain constant (i.e., the ceteris paribus assumption), except the price of the product under study.
- It is assumed that each firm makes decisions in order to maximize profits and that consumers behave in a rational manner in order to maximize their self-interest.

DEMAND (consumers' desire + their ability to buy)

If you were to ask your classmates how many pencils they would purchase at different prices, you would find that, ceteris paribus, they will tend to buy more pencils as the price of pencils falls. This truth is so universally held that economists call it a law.

The law of demand states that the quantity demanded of a product varies inversely with its price.

Schedule 2.1 and Diagram 2.1 show this relationship between quantity demanded and price.

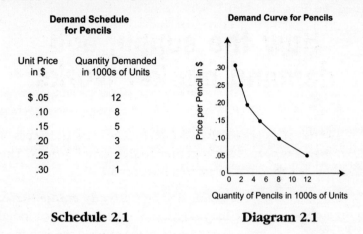

Demand Schedule for Pencils	
Unit Price in $	Quantity Demanded in 1000s of Units
$ .05	12
.10	8
.15	5
.20	3
.25	2
.30	1

Schedule 2.1   Diagram 2.1

Why do consumers behave this way? That is, why do demand curves slope down and to the right?

- The **substitution effect** states that as the price of a product falls (in this case pencils), consumers will purchase more pencils instead of the substitute pens.
- The **income effect** states that as the price of the product falls, a consumer's **real income** (what you can buy with the wages you bring home) increases. Since consumers are now better off, they will tend to buy more pencils.
- The **law of diminishing marginal utility** (MU) states that as a person consumes more and more units of a product, the extra utility (satisfaction) derived from each additional unit is less and less. Therefore, to entice consumers to buy more units the price will have to be lowered. For example, the first pencil purchased will have a lot of utility and, therefore, a person would be willing to pay a high price for it. However, a second pencil will have less utility, so consumers are not willing to pay the same amount as they did to purchase the first pencil. This is why demand curves slope down and to the right.

9

Consumer equilibrium

Consumer equilibrium is an extension of the marginal utility concept. Utility can't be measured objectively but it provides a way to explain consumer choice. A consumer is said to be in equilibrium when the marginal utility (MU) of good A divided by the price of A equals the MU of B divided by the price of B and so on.

$$\frac{\text{MU of A}}{\text{Price of A}} = \frac{\text{MU of B}}{\text{Price of B}} = \dots \frac{\text{MU of Z}}{\text{Price of Z}}$$

When the price of B falls (in this case, pens), the consumer will buy more of item B (pens) and less of A (pencils) to restore equilibrium. By focusing on the addition to total utility that an individual receives from consuming one more unit of that product, that individual can maximize his or her total utility.

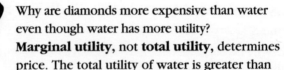

Why are diamonds more expensive than water even though water has more utility?
Marginal utility, not **total utility,** determines price. The total utility of water is greater than the total utility of diamonds, but because diamonds are much scarcer than water, diamonds have a higher marginal utility. Economists call this the **paradox of value**.

Change (shift) in demand

Let's assume something other than the price of pencils changes and the result is an upward shift in the demand curve to D_1D_1 as in Diagram 2.2. In every price range quantity demanded increases by 2000 units:

Factors that can cause an upwards shift in a demand curve include:

- An increase in the price of a substitute good. An increase in the price of pens will cause the demand curve for pencils to shift as in Diagram 2.2.
- A decrease in the price of a complementary good (for example cheaper erasers lead to a greater use of pencils).

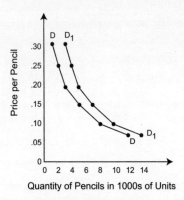

Shift in the Demand Curve for Pencils

Price per Pencil (vertical axis)

Quantity of Pencils in 1000s of Units

Diagram 2.2

- Consumers get wage increases.
- Expectation of higher future prices (for example, pencil makers threaten to go on strike).
- Consumer preferences shift away from other products and towards this product.

By reversing the above five factors, the demand curve would shift downward.

Change in demand versus change in quantity demanded

To understand demand, you must distinguish between a change in demand and a change in quantity demanded. A **change in quantity demanded** – a movement along a given demand curve – is caused by a change in the price of the product. On the other hand a **change in demand** – a shift of the whole curve to the right or left – is caused by something other than a change in the price. See Diagram 2.3 and 2.4.

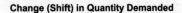

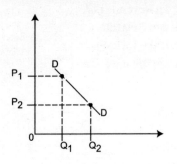

Diagram 2.3

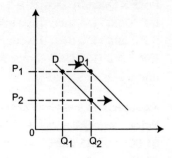

Diagram 2.4

Price elasticity of demand

Virtually all demand curves slope downwards and to the right, but the slopes of demand curves vary. **Price elasticity of demand** is a measure of the responsiveness of quantity demanded to a change in the product's price. If quantity demanded is highly responsive to a change in price, it is said to be price elastic (see Diagram 2.5) and if it is unresponsive to a price change it is said to be **price inelastic** (see Diagram 2.6).

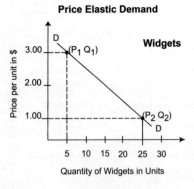

Diagram 2.5   **Diagram 2.6**

Three methods of measuring price elasticity of demand

1.   Price × Quantity Demanded = Total Revenue (TR)
      If P ↑ and TR ↓ then the curve is price elastic
      If P ↑ and TR ↓ then the curve is price inelastic
      If P ↑ and TR remains constant then the curve has
      unitary elasticity

      Example: Widgets (see Diagram 2.5)
      Price ×   **Qd**   =   **TR**
      $1.00 ×   25 units = $25.00
      $3.00 ×   5 units   = $15.00
      Therefore widgets are price elastic in this price range
      since TR fell when $P_1 + P_2$.

2. $E_d = \dfrac{\Delta Q}{\Delta P} \times \dfrac{P_1 + P_2}{Q_1 + Q_2}$ (Note: Δ = change in)

      If $E_d > 1$ the curve is price elastic.
      If $E_d < 1$ the curve is price inelastic.
      If $E_d = 1$ the curve is unitary.
      If $E_d = 0$ the curve is perfectly price inelastic.
      If $E_d = \infty$ the curve is perfectly price elastic.

      Example: Gadgets (see Diagram 2.6)
      $E_d = \dfrac{5 - 10}{\$3 - 1} \times \dfrac{\$3.00 + \$1.00}{5 + 10}$ (Note: Ignore − signs.)

      $E_d = \dfrac{5}{2} \times \dfrac{4}{15}$

      $E_d = 0.67$

      Therefore gadgets are price inelastic in this price range
      since $E_d < 1$.

3.   If you are given percentages to work with, you can measure
      price elasticity using the following formula:

$$E_d = \frac{\% \text{ change in } Q_d}{\% \text{ change in price}}$$

Here is a sample of goods and services that tend to be either price elastic or price inelastic:

Price elastic
- products that have close substitutes
- luxury goods
- goods that are expensive compared to income (example: a new car to most of us)

- goods whose elasticity is measured over a long period of time (for example, consumers adjust to high gasoline prices by buying more fuel-efficient cars over the long term)

Price inelastic
- products that don't have close substitutes
- necessities
- goods that are inexpensive compared to income (example: table salt, a new car to a millionaire)

- goods whose elasticity is measured over a short period of time (example: consumers don't trade in their big utility vehicles for smaller cars immediately after an increase in the price of gas)

Here are some products, with their approximate short-run price elasticity coefficient of demand, listed from the most price elastic to the most price inelastic:

Restaurant meals	1.15	Tobacco	0.38
Magazines	1.10	Gasoline	0.30
Shoes	0.79	Telephone service	0.17

For example, a 100% increase in the price of telephone service will cause the quantity demanded of telephone service to fall by only 17%.

Price elasticity will vary from price to price for any given product. For example, if you calculate the price elasticity of demand for pencils (Diagram 2.1), you will find that the price elasticity varies from 0.6 with reference to prices of $.05 and $.10 to 3.67 with reference to prices of $.25 and $.30. This means that pencils are like most goods – at high prices pencils tend to be price elastic and at low prices they tend to be price inelastic.

Can a demand curve be perfectly price elastic or perfectly price inelastic? It is very rare but there are possible examples. A diabetic who needs a fixed amount of insulin every day in order to live is faced with a perfectly price inelastic demand curve. An individual wheat farmer who is producing a homogeneous product that represents a small fraction of total wheat production is faced with a perfectly price elastic demand curve for wheat.

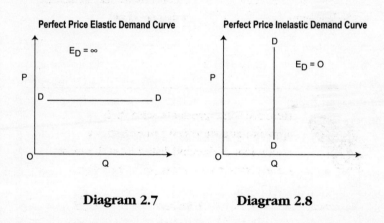

Diagram 2.7   Diagram 2.8

Income elasticity of demand is a measure of the responsiveness of demand to a change in income. Suppose that money income rose by 10% and the demand curves for three different products shifted as in the Diagrams 2.9, 2.10 and 2.11.

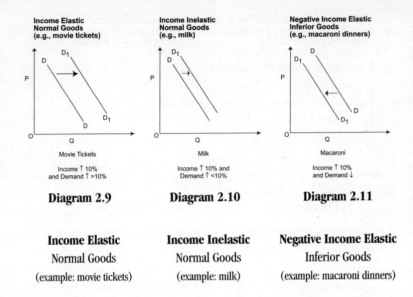

Diagram 2.9   Diagram 2.10   Diagram 2.11

Income Elastic	**Income Inelastic**	**Negative Income Elastic**
Normal Goods	Normal Goods	Inferior Goods
(example: movie tickets)	(example: milk)	(example: macaroni dinners)

As income increases the demand for normal goods will increase either a lot (for example, movie tickets) making the good income elastic, or a little (for example, milk) making the goods income inelastic. In the case of inferior goods like macaroni dinners, an increase in income will cause demand for macaroni dinners to fall, making the good negative income elastic.

Cross elasticity of demand is a measure of the responsiveness of demand for a good to a change in the price of a different good. For example, if the price of pencils increases, the demand for pens will increase while the demand for erasers will fall.

Change in Demand for Pens as a Result of an Increase in the Price of Pencils

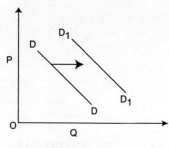

Diagram 2.12

Substitute goods have positive cross elasticities of demand.
The closer the goods are to being substitutes, the higher the elasticity coefficient.

Change in Demand for Erasers as a Result of an Increase in the Price of Pencils

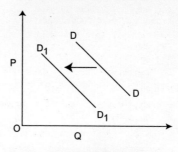

Diagram 2.13

Complementary goods have negative cross elasticities of demand.
The closer the goods are to being complements to one another, the higher the negative coefficient.

Price elasticity has more practical applications than other parts of the theory of price determination. For example, if retailers have an accurate measure of the price elasticity of a product, the correct price to charge to maximize revenue is easier to determine. If a government wants to discourage cigarette sales by using taxes, knowledge of the price elasticity of demand for cigarettes is essential to predict the expected outcome of a tax increase.

SUPPLY

The assumptions made at the beginning of this chapter apply; in particular take note of the assumption about the time period because it is important when dealing with the supply side of the market.

The law of supply states that quantity supplied varies directly with price.

Supply Schedule
for Pencils

Unit Price in $	Quantity Supplied in 1000s of Units
$ .05	1
.10	3
.15	5
.20	7
.25	8
.30	9

Schedule 2.2

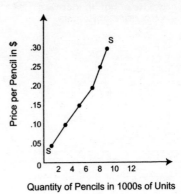

Supply Curve for Pencils

Diagram 2.14

Why do supply curves slope up and to the right?

- At higher prices producers increase output, and new producers are drawn into the market.
- As output increases, inputs will rise in cost because they have to be attracted away from other uses.
- The law of diminishing marginal return provides another reason for the slope (see Chapter 4).

Change (shift) in supply

As was the case with demand, the assumption was made that price is the only independent variable. Now assume something other than the price changes, and the result is an increase in the supply curve to S_1S_1. In every price range the quantity supplied increases by 3000 units. See Diagram 2.15.

18

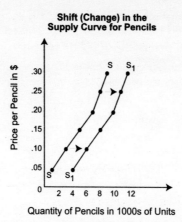

Shift (Change) in the Supply Curve for Pencils

Price per Pencil in $

Quantity of Pencils in 1000s of Units

Diagram 2.15

Factors that can cause an increase in the supply curve include:

- Any factor that causes the cost of production to fall will result in an increase in supply. For example, improved technology, lower levels of taxation and good weather that produce bumper agricultural products all reduce production costs. In the case of pencils, cheaper wood and lower wage levels for workers will cause the supply curve for pencils to increase.
- If prices of other wood products fall, then producers will shift resources into pencil production in an attempt to maintain their income.
- Since market supply consists of the output of all the firms in the industry, if the number of producers increases because of a general increase in economic activity, supply will increase.
- If producers expect higher prices in the future, they may increase output today in anticipation.

Change in supply versus a change in quantity supplied

What holds for the demand curve also holds for the supply side of the market. A **change in quantity supplied** – a movement along a given supply curve – is caused by a change in the price of the product and nothing else. A **change in supply** – a shift of the whole curve – is caused by something other than a change in the price of the product under study.

Price elasticity of supply is a measure of the responsiveness of quantity supplied to a change in price. The TR method can't be used to calculate price elasticity of supply but the other two methods used to measure price elasticity of demand can be used to measure price elasticity of supply.

$$E_s = \frac{\Delta Q}{\Delta P} \times \frac{P_1 + P_2}{Q_1 + Q_2}$$

$$E_s = \frac{\% \text{ change in quantity supplied}}{\% \text{ change in price}}$$

Listed below are the general characteristics of goods and services that have either price elastic or price inelastic supply curves.

Price Elastic Supply	Price Inelastic Supply
• the longer the time period, the more elastic the supply curve • goods with a long shelf life (for example, nails) • producers have a lot of unused capacity • when it is easy to shift resources into making the product (for example, standard computer keyboards)	• short time frame (for example, over one month, the supply of tomatoes is inelastic but over a two-year period, supply will be elastic) • goods with a short shelf life (for example, strawberries) • producers already working at full capacity • when it is difficult to shift resources into making the product (for example, writing complex software programs)

Practice Exercise 2

1. Indicate how each of the following items would shift the demand curve for butter.
   (i)   The price of margarine (a substitute) increases. _____
   (ii) The price of corn (a complementary good) falls. _____
   (iii) Doctors say that butter is bad for your health. _____
   (iv) Average wages and salaries increase. _____
   (v)   The price of butter falls. _____
   (vi) Experts predict a severe milk shortage. _____

2. Product Y increases in price from $5.00 per unit to $20.00 per unit and quantity demanded falls from 6000 units to 4,000 units. Calculate price elasticity of demand for this product using both the TR method and the equation

$$E_d = \frac{\Delta Q}{\Delta P} \times \frac{P_1 + P_2}{Q_1 + Q_2}$$

3. The government levies a new 20% import tax on widgets. Widgets have a price elasticity coefficient of demand of 1.2. As a result of this new import tax, quantity of widgets demanded will _____ (increase/decrease) by _____ %. Widgets are price _____ (elastic/inelastic) in this price range.

CHAPTER THREE

How the market works – equilibrium

In economics, the point where the demand and supply curves intersect is called the **market equilibrium**. This is the price where the amount that consumers are willing to buy equals the amount that producers are willing to sell. Diagram 3.1 below shows that at a price of $.15 per pencil, consumers are willing to purchase 5000 units. This is exactly what producers would be willing to supply at this price. At a market price of $.20 consumers are only willing to buy 3000 units whereas producers would be willing to supply 7000 units. Now the market is faced with a surplus of 4000 units and the price will be under downward pressure to restore balance. Similarly, at any price below $.15 per unit, a market shortage exists and prices will be subject to upward pressure. Thus the term **market equilibrium (E)** – the price to which market forces move to achieve balance.

Diagram 3.1   **The Market for Pencils**

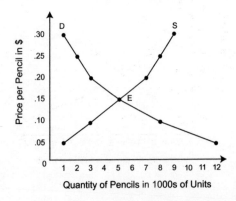

Non-price rationing devices

Complaining about high prices is a Canadian pastime, but if prices were not used some other rationing devices would have to be used. For example, every Christmas there is a toy that every child must have, which usually disappears quickly from store shelves; you, however, know a toy store manager who sets aside the toy for you. If the price system is used in this situation, prices will rise until equilibrium is established and the shortage disappears.

Other examples of non-price rationing devices include:

- being first in line (for example, camping out to get rock concert tickets)
- personal or occupational importance (for example, the PM gets the best seat at a hockey game)
- "need" as determined by a panel of officials (for example, communism)
- ration coupons (for example, butter during WWII)

Equilibrium and shifts in demand and supply curves

Let's assume something other than the price changes. The result is a new supply curve for pencils as depicted in Diagram 3.2. In every price range, pencil producers will bring 3000 more units to the market.

Diagram 3.2 **The Market for Pencils**

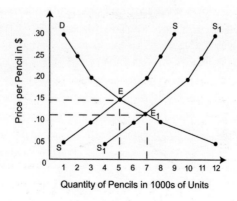

As previously explained, this could be caused by a decline in production costs. Quantity demanded increases from 5000 pencils to almost 7000 pencils. Market price has fallen to $.12 at the new equilibrium (E_1). Note that *demand* did not change because the demand curve did not shift. Similarly, a change in demand would result in a new equilibrium point.

Shortcomings of the market system

The theory of price determination explains how scarce resources are allocated to answer the four fundamental economic questions: what, how, who, how much. In theory the market system is a self-regulating system. As Adam Smith said, it is as if an "invisible hand" were distributing scarce resources in the most efficient manner.

In practice the system has its shortcomings. It assumes that markets are perfectly competitive, but most markets do not fit this mold. A market dominated by a **monopoly** (one seller) will not respond to changes quickly because it doesn't face much competition. While consumers are free to choose, advertising attempts to direct consumer choice.

Since no one owns the air we breathe, the market system offers no rewards to producers and consumers who incur extra costs to keep the environment clean (for example, safe disposal of old paint). The market system is also prone to periods of over-production followed by periods of underproduction – **the business cycle**. Extreme income inequality is another weakness of the system – a sports star earns millions while others who provide valuable services can't earn a reasonable wage.

APPLICATION OF THE THEORY OF PRICE DETERMINATION – FOUR EXAMPLES

1. Price ceilings (rent controls)

Lack of affordable accommodation convinces the government to impose rent controls as illustrated in Diagram 3.3. The government will not allow monthly rental fees to rise above $500 for one bedroom apartments of a standard quality. As a result, quantity demanded increases from the equilibrium amount of 6000 units to 8000 units. Young adults will continue to live with their parents when rents are at the equilibrium price of $650 but when rents fall to $500 the young adults want to say goodbye to mom and dad. On the other side of the market, landlords reduce quantity supplied to 5000 units by converting rental units into condominiums in an effort to protect their incomes. The net result is a shortage of 3000 rental units. Alternative rationing devices end up being used — waiting in line; who you know; key money.

Diagram 3.3   **Market for One-Bedroom Apartments**

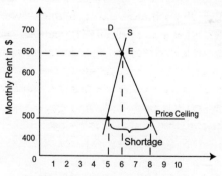

Quantity of One-Bedroom Apartment Units in 1000s

The theory of price determination says that **price ceilings** create market shortages.

25

2. Price floors (minimum wage laws)

The inability of the market to provide a "living wage" to many workers convinces the government to impose minimum wage rates as illustrated in Diagram 3.4. The government will not allow employers to pay anything less than $7.00 per hour to all workers over the age of 17. Employers are reluctant to employ workers at this new wage rate. As a result, the quantity of unskilled labor demanded falls from the equilibrium amount of 10 million hours to 8 million hours. For example, gas stations will switch to self-service. On the other side of the market, quantity supplied increases. Young adults who stayed in school when wages were $5.00 per hour decide to quit school and look for work at the higher wage rate. As a result quantity supplied increases to 12 million hours. A surplus (unemployment) of four million work hours results.

Diagram 3.4

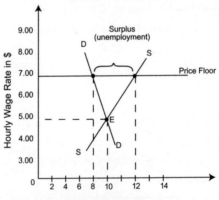

Market for Unskilled Workers

Quantity of Unskilled Workers
over the Age of 17 in Millions of Hours

The theory of price determination says that **price floors** create market surpluses.

3. Who pays the tax levied directly on goods and services?

When a tax is levied, people will try to shift the burden (referred to as **tax incidence**) of the tax onto someone else's shoulders. For example, suppose the government levied a direct tax of $0.05 per pencil at the producers' level. This becomes an added cost of production, which will cause the supply curve for pencils to shift to S_1S_1 as in Diagram 3.5. Prior to the tax, producers were willing to produce 1000 units at a market price of $0.05, but after the tax they will only produce 1000 pencils if they can only get a market price of $0.10 per pencil. The new equilibrium price is $0.17 per pencil ($E_1$). The $0.05 tax per unit results in a $0.02 increase in price, so the producer is forced to absorb $0.03 of this tax. The producer is not able to pass the entire cost of this tax onto the consumer in the form of a $0.05 price increase because pencils are price elastic in this price range.

Diagram 3.5

The Effect of a Tax Increase
on the Market for Pencils

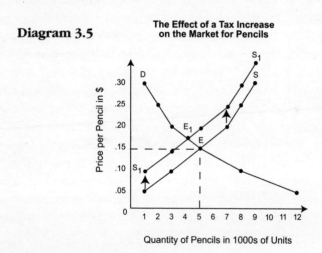

Quantity of Pencils in 1000s of Units

If the demand curve for pencils was perfectly price inelastic, the producer would be able to pass the entire tax on the consumer.

4.   Supply management programs

Low farm incomes have led to government intervention in the market with the goal of improving farm incomes. In the dairy, poultry and egg sectors, the Canadian government has set up marketing boards, which deliberately reduce supply in order to drive prices higher (see Diagram 3.6). If the demand curve is price inelastic, total revenue will increase when price increases. However, if the demand curve is price elastic, total revenue falls when price increases, which defeats the purpose of the marketing board.

Diagram 3.6   **Marketing Boards**

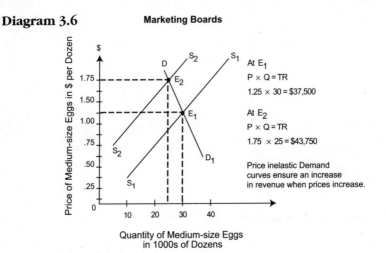

At E_1
$P \times Q = TR$
$1.25 \times 30 = \$37,500$

At E_2
$P \times Q = TR$
$1.75 \times 25 = \$43,750$

Price inelastic Demand curves ensure an increase in revenue when prices increase.

Quantity of Medium-size Eggs in 1000s of Dozens

PROS AND CONS OF THE MARKET SYSTEM

Living in a market economic system, we admire the advantages it offers over alternative systems but we are also aware of its imperfections, including pollution, lack of long-term planning, wasteful consumer spending encouraged by advertising, huge differences between the incomes of the rich and poor and the ability of big business to control markets. However, advantages include the discipline of competition, the wide variety of product choices and the objectivity of the price system as opposed to the subjectivity of other systems. Some view the problems as minor irritants while others see the problems as justification for more government regulations or for making radical changes.

Practice Exercise 3

1. Low wheat prices threaten to force many farmers into bankruptcy. The government tries to help by setting a price floor for wheat of $3.00 per bushel. Diagram 3.7 illustrates the situation:

Diagram 3.7

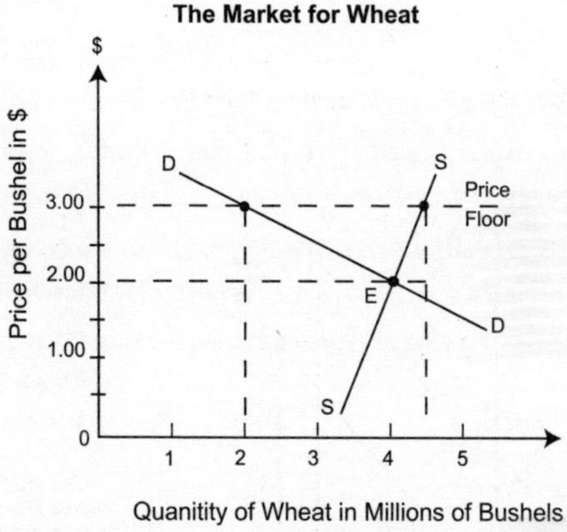

The Market for Wheat

Quanitity of Wheat in Millions of Bushels

Using the diagram, answer the following questions.

(a) Total revenue (TR) for wheat farmers before the price floor is introduced is $ _____ .

(b) As a result of the price floor the quantity demanded will decrease to _____ bushels and quantity supplied will increase to _____ bushels.

(c) The government promises to purchase the surplus wheat and withdraw it from the marketplace. The surplus is _____ bushels and it will cost the government $ _____ to purchase the surplus.

(d) With the price floor, wheat farmers, TR is $ _____ . This amount is $ _____ higher than TR before the floor was established.

CHAPTER FOUR

Theory of the firm

TYPES OF MARKETS

Accountants classify firms by their legal structure – corporations, limited partnerships, sole proprietorships and the like. Economists classify firms by the type of market they operate in: perfect competition, monopolistic competition, oligopoly and monopoly. These are characteristics of the four types of markets.

	Perfect Competition	Monopolistic Competition	Oligopoly	Monopoly
Number of firms in the market	many	many	few	one
Barriers that keep others out of the market (example: patents)	no barriers	existing firms may take action that restricts entry	many barriers	many barriers
Nature of the product	undifferentiated (homogeneous)	differentiated (example: packaging)	differentiated (cars) and identical (natural gas)	unique – no close substitutes
Influence on the market price	price takers	some influence on price but tend to use non-price competition (example: advertising)	significant influence on price; also use non-price competition	price maker
Examples	farming without price support programs	restaurants; beauty salons; retail clothing; car repair shops	car makers; cereal manufacturers; soap producers	public utilities (example: sewage system)

30

Most businesses fall between the two extremes of monopoly and perfect competition. For example, telephone service was classified as a government regulated monopoly but with deregulation, competition has developed. Thus telephone firms now operate in an oligopolistic market where a few firms compete with one another by making their products look distinctive through advertising.

THE COST OF PRODUCTION

Economists organize the decisions that firms make into two basic categories: the short run and the long run. The **short run** is defined as the period in which some factors of production are available only in fixed amounts. For example, if a firm gets a new large order for a particular product, it can hire unskilled labor quickly (variable factor), but it can't get another specialized machine for at least six months (fixed factor). The short run is not equal to a specific time frame. For a barber shop it might be as short as two weeks, but for a steel producer it might be two years. The **long run** is the time period when all factors of production can be varied.

Short run —   Firm has both fixed and variable costs of production.

Long run —   All of the firm's costs of production are variable.

The law of diminishing returns

To understand the cost structure of a firm you must first understand this basic economic law.

The law of diminishing returns says that as more units of a variable factor of production are applied to a given quantity of a fixed factor, the marginal product of the variable factor of production will eventually fall.

For example, Table 4.1 shows what happens when more and more workers, the variable factor of production, are put to work producing widgets with one machine. At first output increases rapidly (increasing returns), but when the fourth worker is added, extra (marginal) production starts to fall (diminishing returns). You might ask why the manager doesn't buy another machine. In the long run if demand keeps up, the manager will buy another machine but this is the short run. It takes months to build another machine. The law of diminishing returns explains why firms face rising costs as they increase output in the short run.

Marginal cost

Marginal analysis is the heart and soul of economic analysis. Marginal means additional or extra. Economic theory assumes that decisions are made by comparing additional benefits with additional costs.

For example, suppose Sue's boyfriend phones her the night before her final economics exam and asks her to go out. Sue says no because she must study. He says that economics must be more important to her than he is. Since Sue has been studying economics she replies, "only at the margin." In other words, the boyfriend is more important when all things are considered, but for the next few hours studying economics is more important. Table 4.1 shows what happens to the marginal product (MP) of labor when additional units of labor are applied to a fixed factor (one machine). Initially the MP rises but eventually diminishing returns sets in and MP falls.

Table 4.1: The Marginal Product of Labor and Diminishing Returns

Labor Input (# of workers) (Variable Factor)	Capital Total (1 machine) (Fixed Factor)	Total Product (# of units)	Marginal Product of Labor	
0	1	0		
			4	increasing returns
1	1	4		
			10	
2	1	14		
			10	constant returns
3	1	24		
			6	
4	1	30		diminishing returns
			2	
5	1	32		

Outside agriculture, perfect competition doesn't exist. Why bother with an economic model that is so divorced from the real world? The answer is that by examining the theory of the firm as it applies to a perfectly competitive firm, it is easier to understand the theory as it applies to other economic markets. It provides an understanding of how revenue and costs determine output. In addition this theory shows how resources would be distributed under "perfect" conditions. For example, in other markets producers use advertising to make consumers believe that there are differences between two products in order to make larger profits. To facilitate this analysis, let's look at a hypothetical perfectly competitive firm that produces widgets.

Table 4.2: Walker Ltd.'s Short-Run Cost Schedule for Widgets.

Output	TFC	TVC	TC	MC	ATC	AVC	TR	TP
500	$16,800	$16,200	$33,000		$66.00	$32.40	$30,000	($3,000)
600	$16,800	$19,200	$36,000	$30.00	$60.00	$32.00	$36,000	$0
700	$16,800	$21,200	$38,000	$20.00	$54.29	$30.29	$42,000	$4,000
800	$16,800	$25,200	$42,000	$40.00	$52.50	$31.50	$48,000	$6,000
900	$16,800	$31,200	$48,000	$60.00	$53.33	$34.63	$54,000	$6,000
1000	$16,800	$39,200	$56,000	$80.00	$56.00	$39.20	$60,000	$4,000

Output This shows the different output levels of widgets that Walker Ltd. can produce and the next six columns represent the costs associated with each level of output.

TC Total cost at different output levels. (TC = Total Fixed Costs + Total Variable Costs)

MC Marginal cost is the additional cost incurred as a result of increasing output by one unit. It is calculated by dividing the change in TC by the change in output. The MC of $20 is calculated by dividing ($38,000 − $36,000) by (700 − 600). (ΔTC ÷ Δ Output)

ATC Average total cost, calculated by dividing TC by output (ATC = AVC + AFC).
MC crosses ATC at its minimum point.

AVC Calculate TVC (TC − TFC = TVC), then calculate AVC (TVC ÷ Output = AVC). MC crosses AVC at its minimum point.

33

MR Marginal revenue is the additional revenue received by selling one more unit of output. In a perfectly competitive market, MR = the market price for the product. The reason for this is that in this market when one firm increases or decreases its output, it will have no effect on the market because this firm sells a homogeneous product and the firm's output represents a very small part of the total market for widgets.

TR Total revenue (MR × output). In this case the market price of $60 is used to calculate TR.

TP Total profit (TR − TC = TP) or total loss if negative.

The MC, ATC and AVC functions from Table 4.2 have been transposed to Diagram 4.1.

Walker's Cost Curves for Widgets for the Short-Run
(Determining Walker's Short-Run Profit Maximizing Position)

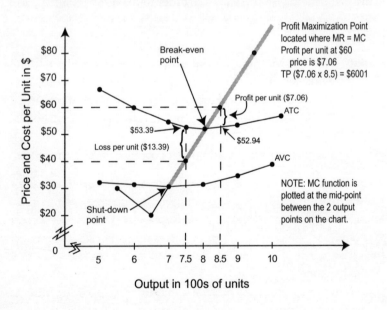

Diagram 4.1

Now that the firm's cost structure is known, the firm will have to decide how many widgets to produce in order to maximize profits or minimize losses, as the case may be. Since this firm and all firms operating in a perfectly competitive market must accept the price dictated by the market (**price takers**), the level of output is the only thing to be decided.

Determining the output at which profit will be maximized, or losses will be minimized

Profit maximization occurs where MR = MC. To understand why, look at the two alternatives. If MR < MC, then the extra cost incurred in producing one more unit is greater than the extra revenue gained from the sale of one more unit. Given that MC varies directly with output and that Walker Ltd can't raise the price of widgets (price taker), the firm should reduce output in order to bring MC into line with MR. If MR >MC, then the firm should increase output. Why? As long as the extra revenue generated by one more unit of output is greater than the extra cost of producing it, the firm should produce more in order to maximize profits.

If MR < MC the firm should reduce output.

If MR = MC this is the profit maximization (minimum loss) position.

If MR > MC the firm should increase output.

Given a market price of $60 per unit (P = MR), the firm should produce 850 units of widgets because at this output MR = MC = $60. Since MC is $60 at output levels between 800 and 900 units the mid point output of 850 is used. The TP column on the chart indicates that profit will be maximized between 800 and 900 units where TP is $6000.

From Diagram 4.1, the profit maximizing position can be located by going up the vertical axis to $60, then moving horizontally to where the $60 line intersects the MC curve. This point occurs at the 850 unit output level. Profit per unit is bracketed on the diagram and total profit can be calculated as follows: (MR − ATC at optimum output) × optimum output. In this case ($60 − $52.94) × 850 = $6001 total profit, which compares to the $6000 of profit from Table 4.2

Break-even point

Instead of a price of $60 per unit, suppose widgets were selling for $40 per unit. MR = MC = $40 at an output level of 750 units. TR is $30,000 ($40 × 750). TP is not a profit but a loss of $10,000 (TR of $30,000 = TC of $40,000 = Loss of $10,000). Although Walker Ltd. is losing money producing widgets at this output level, it is the best output under these circumstances. If it shut down and produced nothing, the firm must still pay its fixed costs of $16,800. If this market situation persisted into the long run, and Walker couldn't lower its cost structure, it would shut down and get out of the business of producing widgets. Walker Ltd can't raise the price because this firm is a price taker. In other words, in addition to being the profit maximization point, the MR = MC point is also the loss minimizing point when the market price is between the break-even point and the shut-down point. At any market price below where MC intersects ATC (also where ATC is at a minimum), this firm will lose money no matter what output it selects.

Break-even point
Where MC intersects ATC
(where ATC is at a minimum)

Shut-down point

Suppose the market price for widgets falls further, to a price of $20.00 per unit. MR = MC = $20 at an output of 650 units. TR is $13,000 (650 × $20) and TC is $37,000, which produces a loss of $24,000. Since Walker's fixed costs are $16,800, the firm should shut down immediately in order to minimize losses. At any market price below the point where MC intersects AVC or where AVC is at a minimum (in this case $30.29) a firm should shut down immediately.

Shut-down point
Where MC intersects AVC
(where AVC is at a minimum)

Economic profits

Accountants calculate the profits of a firm by subtracting the explicit costs of production from revenue generated by the sale of the product. **Explicit costs** are the clearly expressed costs of production such as wages, raw material costs and interest charges on bank loans. Economists, however, calculate **economic profit** by subtracting both explicit and **implicit costs** from revenue. A firm's implicit costs are the opportunity costs of all the inputs. For example, the money invested in plant machinery could have been invested in bonds, which would have generated income with little risk attached.

Economic profit =
Revenue – Explicit Costs – Implicit Costs

Normal profit occurs when economic profit is zero. The implicit costs when added to the explicit costs add up to the profits a firm would *normally* receive if it were fairly paid for the use of its resources, thus the name "normal profits." For example, in the case of the Walker firm (refer to Diagram 4.1), at the widget market price of $60, Walker is making an economic profit of $7.06 per unit. At a market price of $52.50 per unit (Walker's break-even point), Walker's economic profit is zero, but Walker is making a normal profit.

The market supply curve

The market supply curve described in Chapter 2 represents the sum total of all the MC curves of all the firms like Walker who produce widgets. Note that on Diagram 4.1 the MC curve from where MC cuts AVC upwards is drawn with a thicker line to emphasize that this represents Walker's short-run supply curve. At market prices below the point where AVC cuts MC, Walker will shut down so the supply curve doesn't extend below this point.

> MC (Walker) + MC (firm X) + MC (firm Y) + …
>
> = Market Supply Curve

Long-run supply in a perfectly competitive market

In the long run, all costs of production are variable, so the law of diminishing returns is not the compelling force it is in the short-run time period. In the long run, firms move into and out of a particular industry and each firm is able to adjust the scale of its operation. In the long run each perfectly competitive firm will be operating at its most efficient point – the minimum point of its long-run average total cost curve (LRATC). See Diagram 4.2. Market forces will nudge the market price to a point where each firm's **economic profits** are zero. Consequently, in the long run each firm earns **normal profits** but not economic profits.

Diagram 4.2 — Long-Run Equilibrium for a Firm in a Perfectly Competitive Market

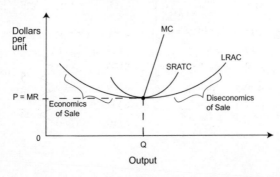

Diminishing returns is a distinctive characteristic of the short-run time period because in the long run the fixed factor will become variable eliminating the problem of diminishing returns. In the long-run firms experience increasing returns as the whole scale of their production process expands. This is referred to as **economies of scale.** However, even in the long run, diminishing returns will eventually set in. For example, there is an optimum size for a car assembly plant – it can get too big to be manageable. Economists call this **diseconomies of scale**.

Monopoly and marginal cost analysis

Analysis of this market is similar to the section just completed on perfect competition in that ATC, AVC, AFC, MC are constructed in the same fashion, the law of diminishing returns applies with the same force and profit maximization occurs where MR = MC. However, this market does have unique characteristics as described at the beginning of this chapter. Each perfectly competitive firm's demand curve is a horizontal line and market price always equals MR. In contrast to this, a monopoly firm's demand curve is a downward sloping demand curve. Thus a monopoly's MR declines with each increase in output. The monopolist is a price maker in that it searches the market demand curve for the spot where it can maximize profit.

Table 4.3 depicts the costs, revenues and profits of a monopoly at different output levels. The numbers from the chart have been transposed to Diagram 4.3.

Table 4.3: A Monopoly Firm – Costs, Revenues and Profits

Output	Price	TR	MR	TC	ATC	MC	Mon P
10	$ 11	$110		$ 80	$8.00		30
			9			4	
20	$ 10	$200		$120	$6.00		$ 80
			7			3	
30	$ 9	$270		$150	$5.00		$120
			5			5	
40	$ 8	$320		$200	$5.00		$120
			3			10	
50	$ 7	$350		$300	$6.00		$ 50
			1			15	
60	$ 6	$360		$450	$7.50		($110)

Diagram 4.3   **Determining the Profit-Maximization Point for a Monopoly**

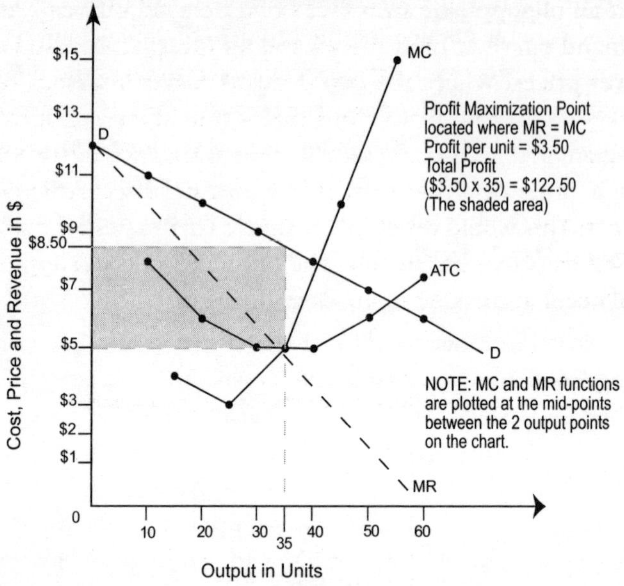

Profit maximization will occur at an output of 30 to 40 units where MR = MC = $5.00 and the demand curve indicates that the monopoly can charge $8.00 to $9.00 per unit for the product. The monopoly is able to earn an economic profit of $3.00 per unit (from the table) or $3.50 per unit (from the graph). The discrepancy in profit per unit is due to the fact that the MR and MC functions are plotted at the midpoints between two output levels.

Oligopolistic firms and marginal cost analysis

Economists have a clear idea about general characteristics of this market, but they are not clear on the details. The **cartel theory** and the **kinked-demand curve theory** illustrates the problem. A **cartel** is an organization of producers who set prices and output levels. The Organization of Petroleum Exporting Countries (OPEC) is an example of a cartel. If oligopolistic firms ban together in a cartel they act like a monopoly; hence their profit maximization point is determined in the same manner as the process described above.

The **kinked-demand curve theory** is based on the premise that an oligopolistic firm faces two demand curves – an elastic demand curve at high prices and an inelastic demand curve at lower prices. Where the two demand curves intersect, the curve makes an abrupt change in slope – thus the term "kinked." See Diagram 4.4. If an oligopolist increased its price beyond P on the graph, other firms in the market would not necessarily raise their prices. This would result in a dramatic fall in sales for the firm that raised its prices unilaterally. The MR = MC rule still applies, and it will occur at the kink in the demand curve.

Diagram 4.4

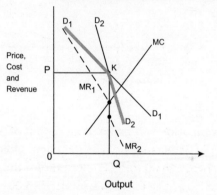

An Oligopolistic Firm
Kinked-Demand and Profit Maximization

Monopolistic competition and marginal cost analysis

Firms operating in this market face a downward sloping demand curve similar to a monopoly because individual firms differentiate their product from the competition. Firms search out the price that will allow them to produce an output where MR = MC exactly as a monopoly does, but their price search is much more restricted because of competition. Since there are few barriers to entry, economic profits will fall to zero in the long run, unlike a monopoly where economic profits will continue indefinitely.

Practice Exercise 4

A perfectly competitive firm produces and sells gadgets at $30 per unit. To answer the four questions, you will need to complete sections of the table for gadget costs.

Output	TFC	TC	MC	ATC	AVC
0	$83	$ 83			
1	$83	$ 86			
2	$83	$ 87			
3	$83	$ 90			
4	$83	$ 95			
5	$83	$103			
6	$83	$120			
7	$83	$140			
8	$83	$165			
9	$83	$195			
10	$83	$235			

1. Calculate the output level of gadgets that this perfectly competitive firm should select in order to maximize profits at a market price of $30 per unit. Explain how you arrived at your answer.

2. Calculate this firm's total profit at its profit-maximizing point. Explain your answer.

3. At what market price will this firm break even? Explain your answer.

4. At what market price will this firm shut down? Explain your answer.

CHAPTER FIVE

GDP and economic growth

So far, we've dealt with microeconomics – the behavior of firm and consumer. Now let's turn to macroeconomics – the big picture. The three most commonly used measures of macro-economic activity are the inflation rate, the unemployment rate and the rate of economic growth as measured by the **Gross Domestic Product (GDP)**.

GDP data gathered by Statistics Canada provides economists with their most important source of information. GDP is defined as the total value at *market prices* of all *final* goods and services *produced domestically* in a year.

Each of the *italicized* parts of the GDP definition need an explanation. **Market prices** are used to measure value because dollar value is the only common yardstick that allows us to add together everything produced, from cars to guitar lessons to the sandwich you bought for lunch. Thus the total number of the millions of goods and services produced are **aggregated** (a number of separate things brought together in a group) using their dollar value as a common denominator. Rather than saying the economy produced one million sandwiches last year, statisticians say the economy produced two million dollars' worth of sandwiches last year.

Only *final* goods and services are counted in order to avoid counting the same item over and over again. For example, an apple farmer sells a bushel of apples to an cider producer for $6. The apples are turned into jugs of cider and sold to a grocery store for $15. The grocery store sells cider in four litre jugs for a total of $20.

If the statisticians added together the $6 sale of apples, the $15 sale of cider to the grocery store and the $20 sale to consumers, the apples would be counted three times. Hence only the final sale of the cider to consumers is counted. But what is to be done with a bushel of apples sold to the cider producer for $6 if at year's end the apples are sitting in a bushel basket awaiting processing and haven't been sold as a final good? In this case the $6 value of the apples will be added to this year's GDP. Goods of this type are called **intermediate goods** and are added to GDP as an inventory item. Therefore, final goods and services for GDP purposes are defined as products that are not sold again before the end of the year. Early the next year the apples are turned into cider and sold for $20. The amount added to GDP for the next year will not be $20 but rather the value added ($20–$6 = $14). Value added, rather than total value, eliminates the problem of multiple counting when dealing with intermediate goods.

Only goods and services *produced* during a given year will be counted. For example, Joe was given a $1500 trade-in allowance on his old car when he bought a new one. The car dealership cleaned the old car and resold it for $2200 in 1999. The value added, in this case $700, will be included in the GDP for 1999.

GDP has replaced Gross National Product (GNP) as the common international yardstick of economic growth. GDP includes all *domestic* production regardless of who owns the factors of production whereas GNP includes all production by Canadians inside and outside Canada. For example, GDP includes the production, of US-owned firms operating in Canada, whereas GNP does not. GNP includes the production of Canadian owned businesses operating in the U.S. whereas GDP does not.

MEASURING GDP

The production of output generates income. When you produce a good or service, you will receive an income when someone purchases the good or service. Every dollar spent by someone represents someone else's income. Therefore, if you want to measure the total production of an economy, you can do it by either adding up total income (referred to as GDP on the income side or National Income) or by adding up total expenditures (referred to as GDP on the expenditure side or Gross National Expenditures). In theory the two methods will produce the same grand total, but in practice the two numbers do not exactly match. Statistics Canada adjusts for the error and produces one number for GDP.

Diagram 5.1 shows the economy with the flow of money ($) moving clockwise and the flow of goods and services and the factors of production moving counterclockwise. If counters were installed at the points where GNE and NI have been inserted on the diagram to measure the number of dollars flowing by for an entire year, the two totals will be the same and this number will be the money value of GDP for the year. This is an oversimplification of the process but it shows that GDP is a flow concept and that total expenditures (GNE) is equal to national income (NI).

Diagram 5.1   Circular Flow of the Economy

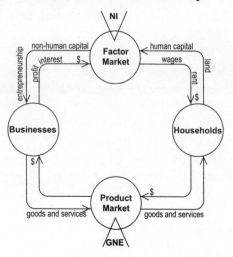

The flow of expenditures approach (GNE)

Consumption (C) expenditures are the largest component of GNE. This includes consumer expenditures on final goods and services produced during the year. Since the object is to measure current production, not all consumer spending is counted. Spending on items produced in prior years is not counted. As well, **transfers** are not counted. For example, if your grandmother gives you $100 as a birthday gift it will not be counted for GDP purposes because no good or service was produced in exchange for the $100 transfer. If you spend the money on CDs, it will then be added to GDP.

Investment expenditures (I) include spending on capital goods and services such as industrial robots and the knowledge to program the robots. Some of the spending will be used to replace worn-out capital and it is called the capital consumption allowance (or depreciation) and the rest is used to buy new (net) investment. (Gross Investment – Capital Cost Allowance or Depreciation = Net Investment.)

GDP counts gross investment such as spending on new homes. In addition, investment spending includes net inventory accumulation. This could be negative if end-of-year inventories are lower than inventories at the start of the year. A firm's inventory includes inputs that haven't been turned into final goods and final goods that haven't been sold at year-end. The value of inventory of final goods at year-end is calculated on the basis of what it is expected to sell for.

As was the case for consumption, transfers are excluded from investment expenditures. For example, if Joe buys 100 common share of Nortel on the Toronto Stock Exchange, we call this an investment but it is not an investment for GDP purposes. In Joe's case there was an exchange of money for common shares. There was no investment in real capital such as the purchase of new trucks; hence it is not counted.

Government expenditures (G) include all levels of government spending on the production of goods and services. Examples include spending on the salaries of civil servants, road maintenance and the cost of running the courts and police departments. Since the largest portion of government spending consists of transfers like unemployment benefits and old age pensions, the largest portion of government spending doesn't appear in GDP.

Since each component of GNE includes some spending on goods and services made outside Canada, imports (M) into Canada are subtracted. By the same line of reasoning, exports (X) are added. The foregoing can be summed up by the following equation:

$$GNE = C + I + G + (X - M)$$

The flow of income approach (NI)

GDP can also be determined by aggregating all incomes earned in a year in the form of wages, profit, rent and interest. Wages include all employee compensations such as health-care premiums and payroll taxes paid on behalf of employees. Business profit includes both the profits retained by business and profits distributed to shareholders as dividends. Rental income includes rent paid for accommodation. Interest income includes interest earned on loans. Income received as transfers such as employment insurance benefits are not included.

As indicated in Diagram 5.2, indirect taxes and depreciation are added to NI to get GDP. Indirect taxes such as the GST are included when calculating GDP using the flow of expenditure approach since the tax is part of the market price. However, indirect taxes do not appear when aggregating incomes to calculate NI, so they are added as a separate item. Depreciation expenditures appear in the flow of expenditures approach and depreciation expenditures represent income in the flow of income approach but this income is cancelled out because depreciation expenditures decrease profits. Thus depreciation is added back on as a separate item.

Diagram 5.2   **Calculating GDP**

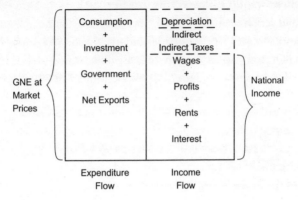

Nominal GDP and real GDP

Since GDP is measured in terms of current market prices and since price levels generally rise over time (**inflation**), GDP will rise even when there is no increase in production. To eliminate the effect of price level changes, GDP statisticians measure GDP using prices from a base year. **Nominal GDP** is measured in current prices whereas **real GDP** is measured in the constant dollars of the base year as in Table 5.1:

Table 5.1: Nominal and Real GDP for Canada in billions of Dollars (1992 = 100) (Source: Stats Can.)

Year	Nominal GDP	Real GDP	GDP Deflator
1992	699	699	100.0
1994	768	749	102.6
1996	834	782	106.6
1998	896	838	106.9

$$\text{Real GDP} = \frac{\text{Nominal GDP}}{\text{GDP price Deflator} \times 100}$$

Unfortunately, eliminating the problem of fluctuating price levels causes another problem. For example, suppose Sally bought a new car in 1992 for $15,000 and she replaced it with a new version of the same car in 1999 for $25,000. If 1992 is used as the base year to calculate real GDP for 1999, the statisticians will add $15,000 to 1999's GDP and assume the $10,000 price increase was caused by inflation. But this ignores quality improvements like improved fuel economy and safety features. If half of the price increase is due to quality improvement and half is due to inflation, the statisticians should add $20,000 to real GDP for 1999 rather than $15,000. Measuring quality improvements is hard to do given the millions of products that statisticians have to measure.

Production that is left out of GDP

- Illegal activities such as the drug trade and prostitution are not counted in GDP.
- Production that does not generate an income flow is omitted. For example, unpaid housework is not counted.
- Cash transactions and bartering are sometimes used to evade taxes. Activity such as this in the underground economy is not included in GDP.

Measuring the standard of living with GDP data

An increase in GDP means that the economy is producing more, which should mean the average standard of living is rising. However, if population increases faster than GDP, the standard of living will fall. Thus GDP per capita is a better measure of the trend in living standards. But even GDP per capita can be misleading if a larger portion of the population is in the workforce. For instance, with more two-income families, GDP per capita may rise but the average living standard may be lower. The best measure of the trend in living standards is the average output per employed person or **labor productivity**. It is calculated by dividing GDP by the number of employed persons.

Just how good is GDP data at measuring anything accurately?

Economic growth increases our living standard by providing benefits like more leisure time, longer life expectancy and a reduction in the need for manual labor. But none of these things are measured by GDP. Double counting, product quality changes, keeping transfers out of GDP and the numerous items produced that are omitted from GDP makes a person wonder whether the GDP number has any validity. Despite these problems, there is a direct correlation between changes in economic activity and changes in GDP, which is very useful information. For example, if the rate of increase in GDP starts to fall, policymakers may be able to take action before growth turns negative and the economy ends up in a **recession**. *Determining the rate of change in economic growth is what makes calculating GDP a worthwhile exercise.*

ECONOMIC GROWTH

Economic growth occurs when real GDP per capita increases over a period of several years. Economic growth also occurs when the productive capacity of the economy increases. For example, discovering more oil reserves in Alberta, building more car assembly line plants in Ontario and allowing skilled immigrants to enter Canada increases the productive capacity of the economy. Economic growth also occurs when labor productivity increases. For example, a restaurant may increase productivity by redesigning the kitchen and by adopting a better training program for the waiters. Increasing production capacity is about expanding the *quantity* of the factors of production whereas increasing productivity is about improving the *quality* of existing factors.

Sources of economic growth

Factors that focus on the *quality* of resources (productivity):

- Invention, innovation and diffusion of new technology. For example, more and more households and businesses are "online," which gives them access to information from millions of locations immediately.
- Investment in human capital. Work experience and formal education make the labor force more productive.

Factors that focus on the quantity of resources (productive capacity):

- Increase the size of the labor force. For example, Canada could encourage the immigration of skilled workers.
- Invest in capital goods. Building better schools and highways and adding new industrial robots to an auto maker's assembly line are example of investments that will increase productive capacity. Economies that devote too many resources to consumption at the expense of saving and investing in capital goods will experience lower growth rates in the future.

Costs of economic growth

- Environmental pollution is a byproduct of economic growth. More cars, more factories and more waste dumps are a result of economic growth. Some say that zero economic growth is the solution. Others say robust economic growth provides the incentive and the wealth to pay for innovations that reduce pollution.
- Since the world has a fixed amount of natural resources, economic growth is limited. Less growth means we will be able to make our resources last longer. Others say the market can handle this problem. When a resource is in short supply, the price goes up and entrepreneurs invest in scientific research to find a less costly substitute or to find ways to use the resource more efficiently. For example, when the price of electricity increased, along came a more energy-efficient light bulb.
- The loss of current consumption is a cost of economic growth. To grow in the future an economy must invest today, so the opportunity cost of growth is the loss of some current consumption. For a poor economy that must devote all of its resources to meet immediate needs, the opportunity cost of growth is very high.

Benefits of economic growth

- A sustained period of economic growth is the best way to increase the average standard of living.
- Higher growth rates usually mean lower rates of unemployment. During the 1930s in Canada, economic growth was negative for many years and the unemployment rate reached 30%.
- Reducing poverty is much easier to achieve when there is economic growth. With zero growth, the only way to help the poor is to take wealth away from other income groups. With positive growth, it is possible to redistribute more income to the poor without lowering the income of other groups.

Practice Exercise 5

Using both the expenditure approach (GNE) and the income approach (NI), calculate GDP from the information provided.

Exports 12	Net interest and rental income 3
Gross investment . . .21	Government expenditures on goods and services 30
Indirect taxes 2	Corporate profits before taxes 17
Depreciation 13	Employee compensation 52
Imports 15	Incomes of unincorporated businesses 6
Transfer payments . .7	Personal expenditures 45

GNE = _____ NI = _____

GDP = NI (_____) + _____ + _____

CHAPTER SIX

Inflation, unemployment and the business cycle

Economist say **economic instability** occurs when the economy is not growing, when the unemployment rate is high and/or when there is a high rate of inflation. Let's consider each of these factors.

INFLATION

In a market system, prices are continually moving up and down in response to various market conditions. This is not inflation. **Inflation** occurs when *overall* prices rise. Creeping to moderate inflation has characterized the Canadian economy throughout the twentieth century with the exception of the 1930s when Canada had a serious deflationary problem. A falling price level is called **deflation**.

Measuring the rate of inflation

There are two ways to measure inflation: the GDP price deflator mentioned in the last chapter and the Consumer Price Index (CPI). The CPI measures the percentage increase in final prices that has occurred in a basket of goods and services since a designated base period. For 1999, the base period is 1992 and the items in the basket of goods and services are based on a 1996 survey of consumer spending patterns. The CPI is a weighted average based on the 1996 survey (in Table 6.1 the weights are in brackets). Out of every $100 of disposable income, the targeted survey group spent $17.90 on food and so on. If prices in both shelter and health and personal care increase by 10%, the increase in shelter costs will increase the CPI 5.83 (26.8 ÷ 4.6) times as much as the increase in health and personal care because people spend more on rent than on personal care.

Table 6.1: Canada's CPI (1992 = 100)

	Sept. 1998	Sept. 1999
All items	108.6	111.4
Food (17.9)	108.3	109.8
Shelter (26.8)	103.6	105.6
Household operations and furnishings (10.8)	108.5	109.5
Clothing and footwear (6.3)	104.4	107.2
Transportation (19.0)	119.9	127.0
Health and personal care (4.6)	108.5	110.6
Recreation, education and reading (11.2)	119.0	122.4
Alcoholic beverages and tobacco products (3.5)	93.2	94.6

Since January 1,1992, the CPI has increased 11.4%. From September '98 to September '99 the CPI has increased 2.6% (111.4 – 108.6 ÷ 108.6). The CPI measures price changes as they relate to the "average" consumer, which means that if you are not average the number is a bit misleading. For example, every September tuition fees are taken into account and 1999 saw a big increase in these fees. But if your household didn't have anyone attending college the tuition fee increase wouldn't affect you. Despite the shortcomings the CPI does a good job of measuring the *trend* in the price level.

CAUSES OF INFLATION

Demand-pull inflation occurs when the total demand for products in the whole economy – aggregate expenditures (AE) – is greater than total supply. This causes the price level to rise. It is caused when the GNE components, C, I, G, (X-M) increase to the point where actual GNE (GDP) > potential GDP. The inflationary gap in Diagram 6.1 depicts this situation. It could be triggered by rising consumer confidence.

Cost-push inflation occurs when energy, wages and other factors of production increase in cost. Producers then pass the higher costs onto the consumer. However, if the increase in the cost of production is matched by an increase in productivity, there is no upward inflation pressure.

The **money supply** is the only real cause of inflation according to **monetarist** economists. They say that inflation occurs when money loses its value, which happens when the money supply grows faster than the production of goods and services. Monetarists say that the money supply should only grow at a rate equal to the long-term trend in potential GDP. Non-monetarists acknowledge that the money supply is important but it is not the exclusive cause of inflation. If inflation is caused by a shock (for example, OPEC reduces oil production by 3 million barrels per day), price levels will rise and then stabilize as long as the money supply holds steady. However, if the money supply increases as world oil prices increase, inflation will continue. In an inflationary environment everyone gets conditioned to expect more inflation. For example, producers increase the price of their products at regular intervals and consumers accept the higher prices because they have negotiated regular **cost of living allowance (COLA)** adjustments to their wages to offset the effects of inflation. An inflationary spiral takes hold, fed by an ever-expanding money supply.

Living with inflation

Some argue that a small amount of inflation acts as an economic stimulant. It encourages spending, which keeps the economy growing and the unemployment rate low. However, if creeping inflation is not stopped it can lead to runaway inflation and runaway inflation can destroy an economy as it did to Germany in the 1920s. Hyperinflation destroys the money system, so people revert back to barter and a modern economy can't function efficiently using barter. If Canada's rate of inflation is greater than the rate of inflation in the United States, export sales will fall and the Canadian dollar will depreciate. This in turn will accelerate the rate of inflation. Non-productive activities replace productive activities as a way of making a living. For example, precious metal is bought, stored and then resold without anything being done with it.

On an individual basis there are winners and losers. Those who anticipate the future rate of inflation may be able to protect themselves. For example, in an inflationary period real estate usually appreciates in value so those who see it coming buy land. Debtors win and creditors lose because debtors repay creditors in dollars that are worth less. Those living on fixed incomes (for example, non-indexed pensions) lose.

Creeping inflation is preferable to deflation because deflation discourages spending. Why buy a new car today when it will be cheaper six months from now? The Bank of Canada's policy is to keep the annual rate of inflation between 1% and 3%.

UNEMPLOYMENT

Stats Canada defines an **unemployed** person as someone over 14 years of age who is available for work and who is actively looking for work. It doesn't include someone who has become discouraged and has given up looking for work or someone who wants a full-time job but has only been able to find part-time employment.

Unemployment Rate = $\dfrac{\text{Number Unemployed} \times 100}{\text{Number in the labor force}}$

The **labor force** is the number of workers who are employed plus the number who are unemployed.

There are four common causes of unemployment:

- **Seasonal** unemployment is caused by changes in the weather. In general there are more jobs available in the warmer months. Canada's unemployment rate is seasonally adjusted so that the unemployment rate better reflects longer-term trends in the labor market.
- **Frictional** unemployment happens when workers move between jobs. In a healthy economy frictional unemployment is high as people move to take advantage of new opportunities.
- **Structural** unemployment is caused by things like changes in technology (for example, bank tellers replaced by ATMs), the depletion of resources (for example, fishery) and when workers skills don't match business needs.
- **Cyclical** unemployment is caused by a decline in aggregate expenditures (AE). For example, if interest rates climb consumers will buy less on credit.

Full employment is *not* defined as zero unemployment. Frictional, structural and seasonal unemployment can never be totally eliminated. Therefore, there is a natural rate of unemployment, called **NAIRU**, even when the economy is operating at potential GDP. Politicians and economists cannot agree on what NAIRU should be but all agree that zero unemployment is unattainable.

Disadvantages of living with unemployment

Those who are unemployed don't have to be told that they suffer both socially and economically. The whole economy suffers because of lost production.

THE BUSINESS CYCLE

Long-term factors like productivity and demographics determine the trend in **potential GDP** growth. Potential GDP measures what the economy is capable of producing if all factors of production are employed at their normal rates of use. For example, an economy would be operating above potential GDP if the normal work week is defined as 40 hours but workers are actually putting in 45 hours per week.

Short-term fluctuations that deviate from the trend are called the **business cycle** and these fluctuations represent actual GDP as opposed to potential GDP. See Diagram 6.1. If potential GDP > actual GDP, a recessionary (unemployment) gap will develop. If potential GDP < actual GDP, an inflationary gap will develop.

A business cycle can be severe like the Great Depression of the 1930s or mildlike the 1991-92 recession. They can be long or short. Despite these differences, a business cycle has four features.

- **Trough** is the term used to describe the bottom of the cycle. Actual GDP < potential GDP. Aggregate expenditures (AE) are low, which causes unemployment to rise. Inflation is usually not a problem. If GDP declines for six months or more, it is called a **recession**, and if GDP continues to decline year after year, it is called a **depression**. The recessionary gap in Diagram 6.1 illustrates this part of the cycle.
- Eventually **expansion** will occur. AE increases, unemployment starts to fall and GDP starts to grow again.

- The **peak** is used to describe the top of the cycle. Actual GDP > potential GDP. AE is too high and inflation becomes a problem. Full employment might be approached. The inflationary gap in Diagram 6.1 illustrates this part of the cycle.
- A **contraction** in economic activity sets in after the peak. AE starts to fall, unemployment creeps higher and the rate of growth in GDP slows. Inflationary pressures ease.

Diagram 6.1　　　　　　　　**The Business Cycle**

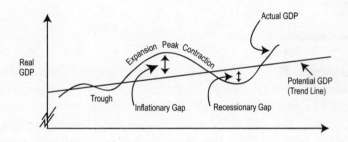

Causes of the business cycle

Short-term fluctuations in GDP are caused by changes in AE, which can be represented by the equation GNE = C + I + G + (X − M). For example, if the United States goes into a recession, exports to the United States will fall and Canada's GDP will fall.

The interaction of investment spending with consumer spending is the source of a lot of the problem. Consider this example of the **inventory cycle**. (Remember inventory accumulation is considered to be investment.) Suppose shoe retailers decide to build up their inventory. Faced with new orders, shoe manufacturers hire additional workers. The new workers rush out and purchase new shoes with their first paycheques. Shoe retailers find that they can't keep their shelves stocked so they place more orders. The whole process is repeated over and over again and the cycle moves towards a peak. At some point consumers will buy fewer shoes but shipments keep arriving at stores. Retailers get overstocked and phone to cancel all further orders. Manufacturers lay off workers and now no one buys shoes and the inventory cycle reaches the trough. Too much spending is followed by too little. In theory, those in charge should build up inventories in the trough when prices are low and let inventories run down at the peak when it is hard to get orders filled. In practice, everyone knows that spending will slow but no one knows exactly when it will happen; hence most people get caught up in the cycle.

The **accelerator principle** is another example of the interaction between consumption and investment that propels the business cycle. Before looking at Table 6.2, you should note these assumptions:

- Capital doesn't wear out so we don't have to deal with depreciation.
- There is no excess capacity in the textile industry. That is, when consumer demand for shirts increases the manufacturer will have to buy a new sewing machine.
- It takes $400 worth of capital (sewing machines) to produce $100 worth of shirts per year. That is the capital-output ratio (the **accelerator**) is 4:1.

Table 6.2: The Accelerator Principle

Year	Consumer Spending on Shirts	Capital stock (Sewing Machines)	Net (new) Investment	Location on Business Cycle
1	$100	$ 400	$ 400	Expansion
2	$400	$1600	$1200	Peak
3	$500	$2000	$ 400	Contraction
4	$500	$2000	0	Trough

The **accelerator principle** states that an increase in consumer spending (income) leads to an accelerated increase in investment. The change in investment = the initial change in consumer spending × the accelerator.

As you can see from Table 6.2, in year 3, even though the demand for shirts increased, the demand for sewing machines fell. In year 4, when the demand for shirts levelled off, the demand for sewing machines fell to zero and all the workers who make sewing machines were laid off.

Closely associated with the accelerator is the **multiplier principle**. An initial increase in spending sets off a chain of spending. The decision to build a new assembly plant results in building contractors being paid for the construction. The contractors will pay their employees and they in turn will spend a portion of their incomes on consumption (**marginal propensity to consume**). Thus, the initial spending increase gives rise to a long chain of spending. The total increase in national income (NI) that results from an initial increase in spending is calculated using the multiplier.

Consumers can do two things with their **disposable income** (income after taxes are deducted). They can either spend it on consumption or they can save it. The **marginal propensity to save (MPS)** is the amount of each extra dollar of income that is saved and the **MPC** is the amount of each extra dollar of income that is spent on consumption. (MPC + MPS = 1). For example, if consumers save 25% of their income MPS = .25 and the MPC = .75.

Now let's see what happens according to the multiplier principle when there is a spending injection of $100 into the system. Note these assumptions:

- As income increases, consumption spending increases.
- The MPS holds constant at .25 as income increases.
- Savings represent a withdrawal (leakage) from the system. That is, there is no intention to spend the money on investments.

Table 6.3: The Multiplier Principle (MPC = .75)

	Income Generated in $
Initial Spending Injection	100.00
Second round of spending (.75 × 100)	75.00
Third round of spending (.75 × $75)	56.25
Fourth round of spending (.75 × $56.25)	**42.19**

The total income generated by the multiplier =

initial spending injection × $\dfrac{1}{\text{MPS}}$

In the above example, an initial injection of $100 of spending will generate an increase in national income (NI) of $400 . The initial injection could be in the form of export sales or new government spending but investment spending is the component of GNE that is most susceptible to a sudden change. If the MPS is lower, the income generated will be higher. The multiplier principle applies equally to the reverse situation where there is an initial withdrawal of investment spending.

The multiplier and the accelerator combine to drive the economy either upwards to a peak or downwards towards a trough. For example, an initial increase in spending results in a much greater increase in NI because of the multiplier. The higher level of NI will generate more consumer spending, which, in turn, will induce more investment because of the accelerator. The higher level of investment will increase NI and so on.

Keynesian theory of national income determination

You will recall from the chapter on economic growth that actual expenditures (AE or GNE) is always equal to actual income (NI). However, *intended* spending doesn't have to equal actual spending. For example, consumers may intend to spend 75% of their income on consumption and save 25%, but they may end up spending 95% of their income on consumption. Intended savings and intended investment aren't going to be equal very often because decisions to save are made by households and decisions to invest are made by businesses.

Before looking at Table 6.4, note these assumptions:

* The economy is **closed** (i.e., no exports or imports) and there is no government. Thus GNE (AE) = C + I.
* Firms intend to invest a constant sum each period.
* Spending decisions depend only on the level of income.
* The price level remains constant.

Table 6.4: Equilibrium National Income

Actual NI (Y)	Actual Consumption	Actual Savings	Intended Investment	Intended AE (GNE)	Pressure NI(Y) to Rise, Fall or Equilibrium
80	70	10	15	85	pressure to rise
100	85	15	15	100	equilibrium
120	100	20	15	115	pressure to fall

The figures from Table 6.4 have been transposed to Diagram 6.2. Recall from Chapter 5 on GDP that every dollar spent by someone represents someone else's income. Actual expenditure always is equal to actual income. Any point on the 45° line represents the equality between AE and NI. The equilibrium (E) level of NI occurs where intended AE cuts actual GDP. When intended AE > actual GDP, as is the case at the actual NI level of 80, NI is under pressure to rise. The opposite situation exists when actual NI level is at 120.

Diagram 6.2 **Equilibrium National Income**

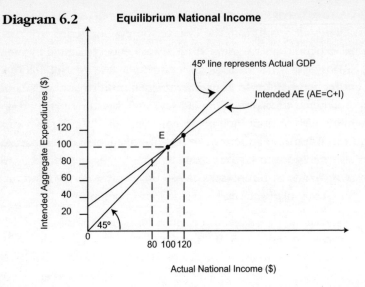

Actual National Income ($)

When the intended GNE (AE) equals actual National Income (NI) the economy is in equilibrium. That is, there will be no tendency for NI to rise or fall. However, disequilibrium is more common so NI is almost always under pressure to rise or fall. This is why market economies are forced to live with the business cycle.

Practice Exercise 6

1. Use the CPI table found in this chapter to answer the following questions.

   (a) What has happened to prices in the alcohol and tobacco subindex since the base year? _____
   (b) Which of the subindexes had the greatest rate of inflation since the base year? _____
   (c) Calculate the percentage increase in transportation from Sept. 1998 to Sept. 1999. _____

2. Assuming that the MPS = .05, calculate the increase in NI that results from an injection of investment spending of $40 million. _____

3. Assume that an increase in NI of $1 per year requires $8 worth of capital. Assume that depreciation is zero. Fill in the table.

Year	NI	Required Stock of Capital	Net (New) Investment
1	30	_____	_____
2	40	_____	_____
3	42	_____	_____

   (a) What is the value of the accelerator? _____
   (b) When the annual rate of increase in NI changes from 10 to 2, net investment falls from _____ to _____ .

4. According to the Keynesian theory of NI determination, what is the basic cause of the business cycle?

CHAPTER SEVEN

Money and banking

What is money? Economist say that "money is what money does." This means that money acts as a medium of exchange, a store of value (saving money to buy birthday presents), a measure of value (comparing the value of items) and as a standard of future payments (loan repayments are set out in money terms). **Liquidity** is money's distinctive characteristic. An asset that can be exchanged for another asset quickly and at no cost is perfectly liquid. Bank of Canada notes (dollar bills) are perfectly liquid because they can be quickly used to buy items and they will be accepted at their face value. Bank savings accounts are less liquid than the bills in your wallet. Your worn-out running shoes are illiquid because they can't be sold. Thus an asset becomes more money-like as it becomes more liquid.

HISTORY OF MONEY

Self-sufficient tribal groups didn't need money. When groups **specialized** – the shoemaker, the stonemason – people had to trade. **Barter** is difficult because rarely is there a direct coincidence of wants (i.e., the stonemason doesn't need a new pair of sandals). There was a need for a trading item that was more widely accepted – something that could be used as money. Cows, cigarettes, playing cards, gold and other items possessing **intrinsic** value are things that have been **monetized,** but they have limitations. Then came a great leap. Money that had intrinsic value was replaced by **token** money. Gold was turned over to goldsmiths (the forerunner of banks) for safekeeping and the goldsmiths issued receipts to the depositors. These receipts circulated as a medium of exchange.

This paper currency was backed by gold, that is, it could be converted into gold on demand.

In the 1700s came the next great leap. Banks began to issue *more* bank notes than the value of the gold they had on deposit. This system worked as long as depositors had faith in banks. When depositors lost confidence in a bank, depositors would demand their gold back (called "a run on the bank"), which might cause the bank to go bankrupt and depositors would be left with worthless receipts. Eventually governments replaced bank notes with their own currency – **fiat money**. Bank of Canada notes are not defined in terms of gold; nor are they backed by gold, they are backed by the Government of Canada. The next step, the one we are presently in the midst of, is the move towards a cashless society. The expanding use of direct debit cards, credit cards, money cards and other electronic transfer systems will mean the end of paper money as the primary medium of exchange.

What gives money its value?

In economics, value is a consequence of scarcity. Scarcity is the result of demand plus limited availability. Factors that keep money scarce are these:

- The economy producing the money is producing goods and services that are in demand.
- The economy is creating money in proportion to the goods and services being produced. Too much and you have inflation; too little you have deflation and a recession.
- Future expectations regarding the demand for and supply of money.
- The money issued has desirable physical characteristics (for example, hard to counterfeit, divisible, portable, easy to recognize).

Canada's money supply includes a variety of assets that are categorized by their liquidity. For example, bank demand deposits are payable on demand (highly liquid), whereas banks reserve the right to be notified in advance for large withdrawals from savings accounts. This is why savings accounts are sometimes called notice accounts.

M1 = Currency outside banks and **demand deposits** inside banks

M1A = M1 + savings **(notice)** accounts with cheque writing privileges + notice accounts of large corporations

M2+ = M1A + all other notice deposits + term deposits + deposits of trust and mortgage loan companies, credit unions and caisses populaires

When the word money is used by economists, they are referring to M1A unless stated otherwise.

Canada's banking system is a branch banking system. Our banks operate under federal government charters and as Canada expanded westward the existing banks opened additional branches. In the US banks historically operated under state jurisdiction and more often than not the local bank was a stand-alone unit. Canada's five largest banks control about 90% of Canada's banking business whereas the US has thousands of banks. The *Bank Act* sets rules on a wide variety of issues. For instance, no one can own more than 10% of the ownership shares of a bank and banks are forbidden from selling insurance directly from their branches. **Near banks** like trust companies and credit unions operate under a different set of rules.

THE CREATION OF MONEY BY THE BANKING SYSTEM

When someone makes a deposit into the banking system, the system keeps only a small fraction of this initial deposit on hand and lends out the rest. Banks are able to do this because:

- Canadians have a lot of confidence in the banking system. We make deposits and know that the money will be there when we want it. If we became disbelievers and rushed to the banks to withdraw our money (creating a run on the banking system), the banks would have to close their doors because the money would not be available. The fact that deposits up to $60,000 are insured by the Canadian Deposit Insurance Corporation (CDIC) helps to maintain confidence in the system.

- The wide use of electronic transfers of money and cheques means that banks don't have to keep much currency on hand. On any given day, the net inflow of currency into a bank roughly equals the outflow, so banks only have to keep a small "float" on hand.

- When someone uses electronic fund transfers (EFTS) or cheques, the money is usually being drawn from one bank account and deposited into another bank account. This type of transaction takes place thousands of times a day. Rather than money physically being moved from one bank to another at the end of the day, all the EFT and cheques are cleared and the net difference moves.

Creating money

Let us start by explaining the process of putting currency into the system. The Government of Canada sells non-interest bearing bonds to the Bank of Canada, and the Bank of Canada buys these debentures with Bank of Canada notes that they have printed. That is, Bank of Canada notes represent government indebtedness to the Bank of Canada. The Government of Canada then puts this money into circulation.

Fractional reserves are the key
to how banks create money.

While currency represents the monetization of government debt, bank deposit money represents the monetization of private debt. This is how it works. To clarify the process we will make three assumptions:

- The reserve rate is a constant 5%.
- The banking system is a closed system. That is, money leaving the banking system quickly finds its way back into the system rather than staying in someone's wallet.
- Banks want to earn maximum profits and they do this by lending out their deposits to the limit of their reserve requirements.

Suppose you make an initial deposit of $1000 in Bank of Canada notes (dollar bills) into Branch X of the Bank of Nova Scotia. The branch will change its balance sheet as illustrated below, using T-account analysis.

Branch X of the Bank of Nova Scotia

Assets		Liabilities	
Reserves	$1000	Demand Deposits	$1000

Branch X of the Bank of Nova Scotia lends out the full limit of the initial deposit (remember the reserve note is 5%) to someone who wants the money to purchase computer equipment. After the transaction, this change takes place on Branch X's balance sheet:

Branch X of the Bank of Nova Scotia

Assets		Liabilities	
Reserves	$ 50	Demand Deposit	$1000
Loan	$950		

Sally, who received the loan to purchase computer equipment has $950 added to her bank account. The bank has created $950 that did not exist before. The bank has monetized Sally's private debt. But there is more. The computer store owner now deposits the money into Branch Y of the Bank of Montreal:

Branch Y of the Bank of Montreal

Assets		Liabilities	
Reserves	$950	Demand Deposits	$950

This branch of the Bank of Montreal will in turn lend out to its limit. When it does, the balance sheet will look like this:

Branch Y of the Bank of Montreal

Assets		Liabilities	
Reserves	$45.25	Demand Deposits	$950
Loan	$904.75		

At this stage the initial $1000 deposit has been turned into $1854.75 ($950 + $904.75) worth of demand deposit money by the banking system by monetizing private debt. This process keeps on repeating itself. The total amount of money that can be created from an initial deposit can be calculated using the **money multiplier formula.**

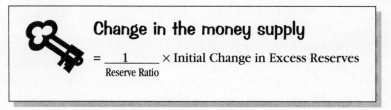

Change in the money supply

$$= \frac{1}{\text{Reserve Ratio}} \times \text{Initial Change in Excess Reserves}$$

In the example above, the initial $1000 deposit with a reserve ratio of 5% can be turned into $19,000 worth of demand deposit money by the banking system.

Change in the Money Supply $= \dfrac{1}{.05} \times [950]$

Thus the banks add to the money supply by making loans. This process can be reversed by the banking system in order to reduce the money supply. In the above example, if the banks call in a $1000 loan the money supply will contract by $19,000.

CANADA'S CENTRAL BANK – THE BANK OF CANADA

The Bank of Canada, a **crown corporation** owned by the federal government, controls the banking system and the money supply and it can protect itself from politicians who might want to manipulate the money supply to gain political advantage. The US calls its central bank the Federal Reserve. To maintain the independence of the Bank of Canada, the Governor of the Bank of Canada is appointed by the federal cabinet for a long term – seven years. Only highly respected bankers need apply for the job. If the federal cabinet doesn't like what the Governor is doing, it has the power to remove him or her. In the early 1960s Prime Minister Diefenbaker and his cabinet removed James Coyne from his position as Governor, but it was a messy process and hasn't been attempted since.

The functions of the Bank of Canada are these:

1. **Issues paper currency**
    - Up until the 1940s chartered banks could issue their own paper notes (for example, Bank of Montreal $10 bill). Today the Bank of Canada has the exclusive right to issue currency.
2. **Acts as the bankers' bank**
    - Chartered banks can borrow funds from the Bank of Canada at the Bank Rate but this rarely happens except in an extreme emergency. Thus the bank is called "lender of last resort." The most important thing to remember about the Bank Rate is that it determines the direction of other interest rates. If the Bank Rate rises, other rates – prime rate, mortgage rates – will also rise.

- The Bank of Canada acts as the central clearing house for transactions among the banks.
- Chartered banks are required to deposit some of their reserves with the Bank of Canada.

3. **Acts as the federal government's banker**
   - The federal government keeps some of its funds on deposit with the Bank of Canada.
   - The Bank of Canada manages the federal government's debt financing. For example, **treasury bill**s (T-bills) are sold by the Bank of Canada to help finance Canada's national debt.
   - The Bank of Canada is responsible for protecting the stability of the Canadian dollar relative to other currencies.

4. **Controls the money supply**
   - The Bank of Canada expands and contracts the money supply by creating and destroying reserves in the same way that the chartered banks create and destroy money by extending and contracting loans. Excess reserves and demand for bank loans are the two factors controlling the expansion and contraction of the money supply. By changing the level of required bank reserves, the Bank of Canada controls the money supply. Let's examine how the Bank controls the money supply by looking at the Bank Rate, open market operations, government deposits and moral suasion.

The Bank Rate

The Bank Rate is the rate of interest the Bank of Canada charges on loans to the chartered banks. The rate is set at approximately one-quarter of 1% above the yield on 91-day treasury bills. By bidding low at the weekly auction of T-bills, the Bank of Canada can push T-bill yields higher. Up goes the Bank Rate. Since the chartered banks rarely borrow from the Bank of Canada, a change in the Bank Rate is used as a signal. An increase in the Bank Rate means that the Bank of Canada intends to slow down the expansion the money supply.

Open market operations

If the Bank of Canada wants to contract the money supply, it will sell government bonds. The person who purchases the bonds will write a cheque on her account with a chartered bank. The Bank of Canada will place the proceeds into an inactive account and chartered bank reserves will no longer support its loan commitments. The banks will be forced to reduce their loans. In other words, the bonds act like a sponge soaking up excess liquidity by destroying bank reserves.

Bank of Canada net seller of government bonds → Bank reserves decline → Money supply contracts → Interest rates rise

Using the money multiplier formula, the sale of $1 million worth of bonds (assuming a reserve rate of 5%) will eventually reduce the money supply by $19 million ($\frac{1}{.05} \times \$950,000$). To expand the money supply, the Bank of Canada will be a net buyer of bonds and each of the above steps is repeated but they move in the opposite direction.

Federal government deposits

The Bank of Canada can move federal government deposits in and out of the banking system. If the Bank of Canada wants to expand the money supply, it will transfer government deposits out of its own accounts and into accounts with the chartered banks. The banks then find themselves with increased reserves and they start to make more loans.

Moral suasion

Finally, the Bank of Canada can try to persuade the chartered banks to take a desired action. For example, if the Bank of Canada wants to expand the money supply, the Bank of Canada will attempt to persuade the banks to ease credit conditions for customers.

In summary, the Bank of Canada's most important function is to control the money supply and the the primary way that it does this is by changing the reserves of the chartered banks through open market operations.

Practice Exercise 7

1. Even though Canadian Tire "money" is a medium of exchange, a store of value and a standard of value, why isn't it considered to be part of Canada's money supply?

2. Assuming the reserve rate is 7%, calculate the potential amount of bank deposit money that can be created from an initial increase in a bank's reserves of $50,000.

3. If the Bank of Canada wants to expand the money supply, it will begin by bidding _____ (high/low) at the next auction for T-bills. This will cause T-bill yields to _____ (rise/fall) which in turn will force the Bank Rate ____ (up/down). Next the Bank of Canada will become a net _____ (buyer/seller) of government bonds in the open market. This action will _____ (increase/decrease) chartered bank reserves and the chartered banks will then be in a position to make _____ (more/fewer) loans.

CHAPTER EIGHT

Conflicting views on fiscal and monetary policy

Economic **stabilization policies** attempt to keep activated GDP near potential GDP. This is where employment will be close to the natural rate of unemployment (NAIRU) and inflation will be in the 1% to 3% range. If we assume that economic instability is primarily caused by undesirable changes in aggregate expenditure (AE) as the theory of NI does, then economic stability can be achieved by getting the government to manage AE. **Fiscal policy** attempts to control AE using taxes and government spending. **Monetary policy** uses control of the money supply to achieve stability.

Diagram 8.1

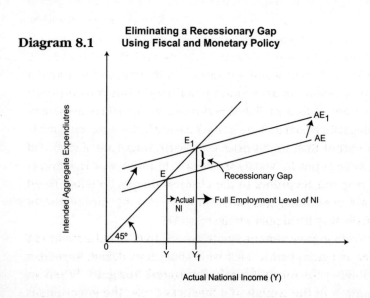

Eliminating a Recessionary Gap Using Fiscal and Monetary Policy

Suppose the economy is operating at point E as illustrated in Diagram 8.1. Refer back to Chapter 6 and the Keynesian theory of NI determination. The actual level of NI at point E is below the full employment level of NI (Y_f) in Diagram 8.1. The economy is operating below potential GDP, which gives rise to a recessionary gap. The objective of fiscal and monetary policy is to shift AE to AE_1 and keep it there. It all seems quite simple in theory, but close examination of the process reveal problems.

FISCAL POLICY

Classical economics dominated economic thought up to the Great Depression of the 1930s. Classical economists like Adam Smith (in the 1700s and 1800s) believed that the market system was self-correcting. For example, if the economy slipped into a recession, market prices would fall and spending would pick up. Businesses would start hiring more workers and the economy would return to equilibrium at the full employment level of NI (Y_f). Consequently government should keep its hands off the economy **(laissez-faire policy)** and simply balance its budget year after year.

In the early years of the Great Depression governments followed the classical prescription, but the economic situation kept getting worse. In response to this problem John Maynard Keynes developed a theory that came to be called **Keynesian economics**. The theory of national income determination in the final chapter is based on the ideas of Keynes. Keynes said that the chronic instability of private sector spending, and in particular investment spending, results in an economy that might not return to full employment on its own. For example, he said that when investment spending falls, which induces a larger fall in AE, firms are more likely to cut output than to cut prices. Similarly, wages are slow to fall or, as Keynes put it, "wages are sticky." In other words, markets don't respond according to the classical theory. So when faced with a recessionary gap, governments should implement an **expansionary** fiscal policy to increase AE.

When a government spends more than it collects in tax revenue in a given year, it is left with a budgetary deficit. Keynesian economics calls for **cyclically balanced budgets**. When an economy is in the trough of a business cycle, the government should cut taxes, increase spending and deliberately run deficits. It should do the opposite in the peak phase of the cycle. Budgetary deficits don't have to be huge in order to be effective because of the effects of the multiplier and accelerator principles. Remember, the principles say that an initial change in spending will result in a much greater change in NI. By manipulating AE in this way government can fine-tune the economy in order to moderate cyclical swings.

Diagram 8.2

Keynesian Cyclically Balanced Budgets

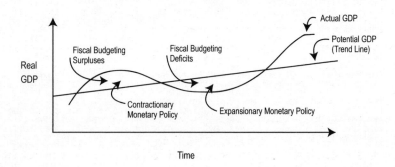

In the Keynesian model there are two types of fiscal stabilizers – automatic and discretionary. **Automatic stabilizers** are built into the system and go into action without requiring enabling legislation. For example, the Employment Insurance (EI) fund is set up to collect more premiums and pay out less in benefits when the economy is at the peak of the cycle. The resulting surpluses build up automatically, withdrawing potential spending from the booming economy. The downside of automatic stabilizers is that they act as a **fiscal drag** on the economy as it starts to expand, slowing down the recovery rate.

Discretionary stabilizers require enabling legislation. For example, as the economy starts to contract the government passes legislation that reduces personal income tax rates to stimulate consumer spending. Another example is public works projects. Major spending on roads should be left to periods of economic contraction, according to Keynesian economists.

Problems with Keynesian fiscal policy

Today, economists generally feel there are four major problems with Keynes's theory. **Time lags** refer to the time between the start of the problem to when fiscal policy begins to have an effect. Gathering data, forecasting accurately, mustering the political will to act, implementing the policy and the period needed for the medicine to start working all add up to a time estimated to stretch from months to years. Keynesian remedies are like taking medicine for an illness you had last year. This criticism applies to discretionary measures but not to automatic stabilizers.

A second problem is that budgetary deficits must be financed and if they are financed by "**crowding-out**" other borrowers, the increase in government spending will only equal the decrease in private investment and consumption. If this is the case, fiscal policy won't expand AE.

A third problem area arises from the fact that in Canada the federal government has the primary responsibility for economic stability but political and social issues are also important. It is difficult to sell a tax increase to the electorate in order to accumulate budgetary surpluses. It is difficult to cut spending on badly needed roads in order to dampen a booming economy. It is difficult for the federal government to tell the provinces how to manage their budgets.

The development of a global economy is the fourth problem area. International flows of capital make it difficult to implement a national fiscal policy. For example, if taxes are raised in Canada, capital will flow out of Canada.

Monetarists argue that time lag and crowding out problems make fiscal policy useless. They agree with Keynesian economists that business cycles are caused by changes in AE but the solution monetarists say, rests with monetary policy not fiscal policy.

Supply-side economists (supply-siders) argue that the focus should be on the supply side of the market. One branch of the supply-side school says that government spending aimed at increasing AE produces nothing but inflation. Strong labor unions, big business, high taxes and government regulation raise costs and make markets uncompetitive. The best way to increase investment according to supply-siders is to increase the desire to save using incentives like tax cuts.

 Keynesians disagree with the supply-siders, view on the need to increase savings. An increasing desire to save will actually reduce saving. Keynesians call it the **paradox of thrift** and it works like this. If *everyone* tries to save more and consume less, AE will fall, which means NI will be lower and everyone ends up with less income to save.

MONETARY POLICY

Chapter 7 on money and banking explained how the Bank of Canada can expand and contract the money supply. An **expansionary monetary policy** occurs when the money supply is growing at a faster rate than real GDP. The increase in the money supply causes interest rates to fall, and this increases spending. A contractionary policy is the opposite. Keynesians believe that expansionary and contractionary monetary policies should be used to moderate cyclical swings in the business cycle (refer to Diagram 8.2). However, Keynesians don't think an expansionary monetary policy is as effective as fiscal policy at pulling an economy out of a recession. They say that, if consumer confidence is low it is tough to convince banks to lend and people to borrow no matter how low interest rates are. Keynesians do think, however, that a contractionary monetary policy works relatively well at dampening a booming economy.

According to monetarists, Keynesian fine-tuned monetary policy is unworkable because of time lags and forecasting errors. Attempting to control interest rates in the short run results in the Bank of Canada losing control of the money supply. The solution, according to monetarists, is to make sure that the money supply (M1A) grows at a rate equal to the rate of growth in potential GDP.

The Phillips Curve

Economist Alban Phillips showed that there was a stable relationship between the rate of unemployment and the rate of change in wages in Britain between the 1860s and the 1950s. This relationship is depicted in the Phillips curve (see Diagram 8.3). The Phillips curve says that there is an inverse relationship between the rate of inflation and the rate of unemployment. When the unemployment rate is near the natural rate of unemployment (NAIRU), aggregate expenditures will be high and there will be upward pressure on wages. This will result in more inflation.

Diagram 8.3

The Philips Curve

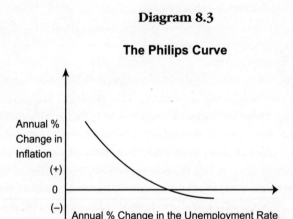

By extension, the Phillips curve is used to suggest that unemployment can be reduced by accepting a high rate of inflation. Conversely inflation can be lowered by allowing unemployment to climb. If this trade-off relationship is still true, it is easy to see the dilemma policymakers face. Opposition MPs are quick to accuse the government of the day of fighting inflation on the backs of unemployed workers.

However, more recent history suggests that this trade-off relationship is not as exact as the Phillips curve suggests. When both unemployment and inflation fall at the same time, as happened in the 1990s, the conclusion is the relationship doesn't exist at all. The rationale for the trade-off is based on the premise that inflation and employment are determined by demand-pull forces. However, if inflation is being caused by cost-push factors like rising gas prices, the trade-off argument doesn't hold up. Costs can push up prices when unemployment is high and any attempt to use unemployment to curtail inflation would be fruitless. The economy ends up with more of both problems – it is called **stagflation**. A typical recession is characterized by negative economic growth, high unemployment and no inflation. Stagflation is similar to a recession, except that there is inflation as well. It is the worst of both worlds.

Supply-side economics

Disillusionment with the Keynesian model forced economists and policy makers to look at alternative theories of NI determination. Supply-side economics became popular in the early 1980s and is sometimes referred to as "Reaganomics" after President Reagan. Supply-siders say that the Keynesian model is based on the idea that economic systems are closed. That is, if Canada were to implement expansionary monetary and fiscal policies to increase demand in the domestic market, it wouldn't matter much if other countries had contractionary policies. The truth is that nearly every country including Canada has an **open economy**. Approximately 30% of Canada's GDP is dependent on foreign trade. In the early 1980s, France tried to use expansionary Keynesian policies to revive their economy but failed.

Since we now operate in a global market place, supply-siders say the focus should be on making an economy competitive in world markets and that means looking at the costs of production. Their aim is to increase economic growth and employment while keeping inflation at bay by improving incentives to savers and producers. We already mentioned the savings part of their policy and the Keynesian criticism — the paradox of thrift. Supply-siders call for tax cuts. Mundell who won the 1999 Nobel prize for economics, says that any tax rate over 30% shifts people's focus from earning income to evading their taxes. A supply-sider by the name of Laffer argues that if governments raise taxes beyond a certain point, total revenue starts to fall because highly taxed individuals and corporations lose their incentive to work, they move to a lower tax jurisdiction or they work in the underground economy where bartering and cash transactions are used to evade taxes.

Diagram 8.4   **Laffer Curve**

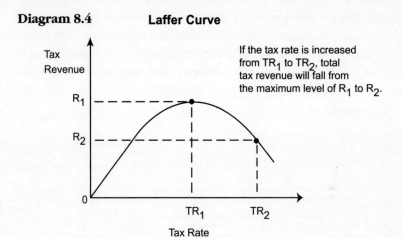

If the tax rate is increased from TR_1 to TR_2, total tax revenue will fall from the maximum level of R_1 to R_2.

In addition to tax cuts, supply-siders call for deregulation, privatization and a reduction in the welfare state. These items will be described in more detail in Chapter 9.

Most economists now agree that Keynesian economics was oversold. Economists and policy makers were too optimistic about their ability to manage aggregate expenditures using fiscal and monetary policies. Monetarists and supply-siders have had a field day pointing out the weaknesses of the Keynesian model. Which of these alternatives offers the best explanation of the business cycle remains an unanswered question.

Practice Exercise 8

1. Draw a graph using a 45 degree line to depict an inflationary gap. Also draw a second AE function and label it AE_1 that depicts the elimination of the inflationary gap. Before doing this question, look at the diagrams in Chapter 6 and the diagram illustrating the recessionary gap in this chapter. Fully label your diagram.

2. What types of fiscal and monetary policies would Keynesian economists use to eliminate an inflationary gap?

3. List three problems associated with Keynesian economic policy aimed at closing an inflationary gap.

CHAPTER NINE

Government
and the economy

The concept of marginal analysis that economists use to examine the actions of consumers (MU÷P) and firms (MC = MR) can also be used to evaluate government. Government can best serve the public interest by increasing activities where the marginal social benefit (MSB) of taking action exceeds the marginal social costs (MSC) of those actions. For example, if the marginal benefit provided by spending an extra dollar on education exceeds the marginal cost of raising the dollar through taxes, then government should spend more on education. If MSB < MSC then the government should reduce its expenditure on education. The problem is finding a way to objectively measure marginal social benefits and marginal social costs.

ECONOMIC FUNCTIONS OF GOVERNMENT

1. **To provide a framework for private economic activity**
    Governments enforce contracts, prevent theft and protect the interests of property owners through the courts. For example, sometimes the market system can't deliver equal knowledge about market conditions as in the case of "insider trading" on the stock market. When the market fails, as in this example, we rely on governments to set rules and enforce them. Governments also test products and provide information on drugs and food in an effort to protect consumers.

2. **To provide certain types of goods and services**
    Goods and services whose benefits flow to everyone because there is no way to exclude those who do not wish to pay are called **collective or public goods and services**. Fire

protection is an example. Suppose one homeowner, Sally, paid a fire hall for fire protection while her next-door neighbor, Joe, decided not to buy the service. A fire starts in Joe's house and Sally phones the fire department to put out the fire because it might spread to her own house. Why should Joe pay when he knows Sally will come to the rescue? In other words Joe is a **free rider**. The only way to stop free riders is to force all homeowners to share the cost of fire protection through taxation. Fire and police protection, national defense, light-houses and weather forecasting are examples of collective goods and services.

Goods and service whose benefits can be partially excluded from free riders are called **quasi-collective**. For example, if Sally goes to college but Joe doesn't, Joe is excluded from the direct benefit of a college education. However the whole community benefits from a better educated population, including Joe. Quasi-collective goods and service tend to be financed by both user fees (for example, tuition fees) and general taxation. Education, roads, national parks and libraries are examples.

Private goods and services whose benefits can be easily excluded from free riders are usually provided by the market. However, there are some cases where the government intervenes. Radio and television broadcasting are essentially private services but the Canadian government provides some service through the CBC for cultural reasons.

Economic progress is dependent on a government's ability to provide good physical infrastructure (for example, roads, sewers, water) and good social infrastructure (for example, public safety, education, health care).

3. **To control monopolies and to increase competition**
Competition is a desirable economic goal because it gives consumers a wide variety of choices, it encourages innovation and it helps keep a product's price in line with the marginal cost of producing the product (the point of optimum efficiency MC = MR). When the market fails to provide adequate competition, government intervention is encouraged.

There are some industries where there is room for only one producer because of the need for economies of scale and the need to avoid unnecessary duplication. This is particularly true for a country with a small population like Canada, For example, the United States has a number of national airlines whereas Canada doesn't seem able to support more than one national carrier. **Natural monopoly** is used to describe this type of industry (for example, sewage systems, electricity, cable, natural gas). Government controls the price of the service either through regulations (for example, cable rates) or through government ownership (for example, electricity). However, governments are currently moving in the opposite direction by deregulating industries (for example, telephone service) and privatizing crown corporations (for example, Air Canada and CN) based in part on the belief that freer world markets will increase domestic competition.

The *Competition Act's* purpose is to prevent anti-competitive behavior. The Act outlaws actions taken by existing firms to keep new firms out of the industry (for example, denying access to raw materials), measures that restrict price competition (for example, oil companies all agree to charge the same price for gas – price fixing) and practices that eliminate existing competition (for example, merging of competitors). The *Competition Act* says that a merger may be allowed if the reduction in competition is offset by economies of scale that produce added benefits to consumers in the form of lower prices or improved quality. For example, in 1998 the Royal Bank wanted to merge with Bank of Montreal and at the same time CIBC proposed a merger with TD Bank. The banks argued that the mergers were necessary in order for them to compete in the global market place. The Competition Bureau argued that any possible benefits from the merger would be outweighed by a reduction in competition if Canada's five big banks were reduced to three. The government rejected the bank merger proposals.

4. **To redistribute income**

   Most Canadians believe that the market fails to distribute income fairly and they want to see poor people helped. As a result governments in Canada intervene to help the disadvantaged.

   Why is it that a NHL hockey player can make half a million dollars in one year whereas a new secondary school teacher can only make $35,000 a year? Economists say that individuals own productive factors or inputs, which economists call **factors of production**. They include land (natural resources), non-human capital (computers), human capital (individual skills) and entrepreneurship (risk-taking). Firms producing goods and services create a demand for these factors of production. Thus we end up with a supply and demand curve for factors of production such as human capital.

Diagram 9.1   **Derived Demand**

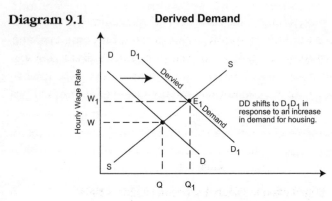

Quantity of Skilled Carpenters

If there is an increase in the demand for new houses, the demand for skilled carpenters will rise. Refer to Diagram 9.1. Thus the demand curve for human capital and the other factors of production is **derived** from the demand for the end product. If the derived demand for the skill that you have is high and the skill is in relatively short supply, the market is going to pay you a lot of money for providing the service (for example, NHL hockey player). If the derived demand for your skill is low and/or there is a large supply of people able to provide the service the market is not going to pay you a lot of money (for example, teacher). The market system can lead to situations that are clearly unfair.

Government attempts to reduce income inequality in a number of ways. Pay equity laws address the problem of gender inequality. Minimum wage laws are aimed primarily at improving the income of young workers. The federal government transfers income from the wealthiest provinces (for example, Alberta) to the poorest provinces (for example, Newfoundland) through equalization payments.

Governments use their tax and expenditure policies to reduce income inequality. The personal income tax and government transfers to regions and individuals do redistribute income from higher-income earners to lower-income earners. Current income tax rates range from 0% for low-income earners to approximately 48% for high-income earners. Refer to Table 9.1 and Diagram 9.2.

Table 9.1

Distribution of Family Income in Canada – 1993
(Source: Stats Canada)

Family Income Category	% of Total Income	
	Before Taxes and Transfers	After Taxes and Transfers
Bottom ⅕	6.4 %	7.7 %
Next ⅕	12.0 %	13.2 %
Next ⅕	17.6 %	18.1 %
Next ⅕	24.1 %	23.8 %
Top ⅕	39.9 %	37.2 %

Table 9.1 is saying that the bottom 20% of Canadian families measured by family income got 6.4% of Canada's total income in 1993 before personal income taxes and payroll taxes were deducted and before transfers were added. But they got 7.7% of total income after taxes were deducted and transfers like EI and CPP benefits were added on.

Tax rates are high, but most of the tax revenue is not being used to redistribute income to the disadvantaged.

The numbers from the first and third columns from Table 9.1 have been transposed to an income distribution curve called the Lorenz curve. The 45° diagonal line on the Lorenz graph represents perfect income equality. The further the Lorenz curve bends away from the diagonal, the more income inequality there is.

Diagram 9.2   **Lorenz Curve**

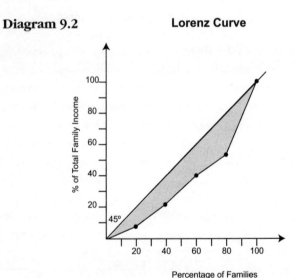

Supply-side economists believe that the best way for government to help the poor is for governments to encourage strong economic growth by cutting taxes. A rising GDP will increase the average standard of living and the benefits will "trickle down" to the poor. They say, "a rising tide lifts all boats." Critics say that the poor don't have "boats," that is, the poor don't have the skills that allow them to participate in the opportunities provided by economic growth. Supply-side critics such as economist John Kenneth Galbraith say that rather than reduce taxes, governments should raise taxes and use the money to provide daycare, housing and education to the poor so they can acquire skills that are in demand.

5. **Economic stability**

   One of the main responsibilities of the federal government is to encourage economic growth with low unemployment and low inflation rates. This topic was covered in earlier chapters.

6. **To reduce the impact of negative externalities like pollution**

   When Sally fixes up the front of her home, she not only increases its value but also the value of Joe's place next door. This is an example of a positive externality. **Externalities** are defined as actions that impose benefits or costs (for example, pollution) on others without their consent. Suppose Joe changes the oil in his car and then dumps the old oil into the creek behind his house. Joe's action has produced a negative externality that is ignored by the market because the creek belongs to no one in particular.

   Governments can use direct controls to cut pollution. For example, government legislated leaded gasoline out of existence. In Joe's case the government could make it illegal to dump toxic waste into creeks and impose fines on offenders. Direct controls, however, tend to be economically inefficient because of the cost of monitoring and enforcing the rules.

   In some cases, governments tax pollution at its source. For example, the government knows that some people will try to get rid of their old oil just like Joe did, so the government imposes a special tax on the makers of engine oil. This action can force the market to go into action. The engine-oil companies may start paying customers like Joe to return the old oil, hoping that the government might then reduce the tax.

Taxing pollution will reduce pollution but it won't eliminate it the way direct controls can. Economists argue that it is impossible to eliminate pollution but it should be reduced to the point where the marginal social cost (MSC) of pollution reduction measures equals the marginal social benefit (MSB) of the pollution reduction measures. Spending beyond this point to where the MSC > MSB results in economic inefficiency.

Whether the government is attempting to control pollution, redistribute income, provide collective goods, create a framework for economic activity or guard against anti-competitive behavior, the key to determining the optimum level of government interference in the market is governed by the economic axiom MSC = MSB.

TAXATION

Governments can use tax policy to fulfill some of the functions outlined in the previous section. Taxes are often called **progressive**, **regressive** or **proportional**. A progressive tax has a rising tax rate as the tax base increases. For example, as personal income rises (the tax base) personal income tax rates rise. On the first $35,000 of personal income, the federal tax rate is 17%, but on the next $35,000, the tax rate jumps to 24%. A **proportional tax** has a constant tax rate as the tax base increases. For example, the GST levies a 7% tax on retail price (the tax base) whether the item sells for $25 or $100. A **regressive tax** has a falling tax rate as the tax base increases. Canada's payroll taxes – CPP and EI – are examples of regressive taxes. The CPP payroll tax takes a constant amount per $100 of income up to an annual income of $37,600 (2000 figures), but then the tax stops. Someone earning $75,200 per year pays the same in CPP tax as the person making $37,600.

Table 9.2 – The CPP Payroll Tax is a Regressive Tax

Annual Income (Tax Base)	CPP Tax ($3.50 per $100 of Earned Income up to $37,600)*	Tax Rate as a % of Earned Income
$37,400	$1,330	3.5%
$74,800	$1,330	1.8%

Characteristics of a good tax

You might be more inclined to say that there is no such thing as a "good" tax. However, if we are going to have taxes, governments should strive to make them as tolerable as possible. Thus economists have come up with some principles for evaluating taxes:

- The more convenient a tax is to pay the better. It is generally more convenient to pay income tax by deductions from your paycheque rather than forcing you to write a cheque once a year for the full amount.

- Taxes should be **equitable** (fair). But what does equitable mean? The **benefit principle** says benefits received should be proportional to taxes paid. For example, the more gas a motorist buys the more benefit the motorist gets out of the roads that are paid for by gas taxes. The **ability to pay principle** says that those with the greatest ability to pay should pay the most. The personal income tax is based on the assumption that annual income is a good measure of one's ability to pay taxes.

- Taxes should be hard to evade. If your neighbor tells you that he only reports half of his income for tax purposes and has never been charged with tax evasion, you might think that you are a sucker for paying all your taxes. Enforcement is important.

- If it costs the government $1 to raise $1 in tax revenue, that tax is too expensive to collect. Income tax collection is cost efficient but toll-road fees are not.

- **Tax incidence** refers to who pays for a tax. Who the government levies the tax on is not always the person who "really" ends up paying. For example, governments make corporations pay many types of taxes and the public thinks the burden of the tax is being shifted away from individuals towards corporations. But in many cases the corporation is able to pass the tax onto the consumer in the form of higher prices. One of the supply-demand applications in Chapter 3 examines tax incidence. When a government levies a tax, it should be clear who really pays the burden of the tax.

THE NATIONAL DEBT

The **national debt** refers to the debt of the federal government. Local governments and the provinces have debt loads as well, but we will focus on the federal debt. When a government spends more than it raises in revenue through a fiscal year, it is stuck with a budgetary deficit that must be financed. This deficit is added to the national debt and the Bank of Canada sells government bonds to finance the deficit.

When you purchase a government bond, you are lending money to the government and the government promises to pay you interest on the loan and repay the principal on the maturity date. Federal government bonds fall into three main categories – debentures, treasury bills and Canada Savings Bonds. **Government of Canada debentures** have maturity dates (the date when the principal and interest must be repaid) that stretch from one to 30 years. They are called debentures because they are **unsecured loans**. No specific government asset is attached to the security as collateral. They trade in the open market, which means that if you buy a bond that matures in 20 years you can sell it before it matures in the bond market. The problem is, if you bought a bond with a **coupon rate** of 6% (the stipulated interest rate) at **par** (the principal amount) and market interest rates climb, you will be forced to sell the bond at a discount (below par). This type of bond carries the greatest risk but also the possibility of the biggest return.

Government of Canada Treasury Bills (T-bills) have maturity dates of less than one year. Since T-bills are issued for a short period of time, holders don't receive interest payments. Instead a purchaser buys at a discount and receives the par value when the T-bill matures. T-bills trade in the open market like debentures.

Liquidity and safety of principal attract investors to T-bills.

Canada Savings Bonds (CSBs) have maturity dates of approximately seven years. CSBs don't trade in the open market but if you decide to cash in before the maturity date, the government will repay the principal plus earned interest. Unlike tradeable debentures, there is no chance of a capital loss. CSBs are unsecured loans (debentures) but like all government bonds, they are backed up by the ability of government to raise taxes to pay them off. Liquidity and safety are attractive features for investors.

There is another way to finance the debt that offers short-term relief but causes long-term pain. When the Bank of Canada sells a bond to an individual that individual must forgo the purchase of something else in order to buy the bond. This represents **real debt** because there is a real sacrifice. If, however, the Bank of Canada buys the government bonds, it is the same as the open market operations described in Chapter 7 that are used to expand the money supply. In other words a government that uses this method is printing money to pay its bills. This is called **fake debt** because no one has to forgo spending money on something else. Countries that resort to paying debts this way eventually end up with annual inflation rates exceeding 50%.

It is all relative

Economist argue that the problem with the deficit isn't so much its absolute size but rather the ability of an economy to pay the interest on the loans. Suppose Sally and Joe each have personal debts of $200,000. Sally's annual income is $100,000 and Joe makes $25,000 a year. Joe is in financial trouble, but not Sally. The same holds for a country.

Whether or not the national debt is having a negative effect on an economy depends more on the ability of an economy to handle the debt service payments than on the absolute size of the debt.

Table 9.3 shows that Canada's federal debt compared to GDP has been all over the map, ranging from a high of 110% in 1945 to a low of 14% in 1975.

Table 9.3 – Canadian Federal Net Debt* as a % of GDP

Year	Net Debt as a % of GDP
1939	38%
1945	110%
1975	14%
1995	71%
1999	64%

*Gross Debt Less Government Assets (for example, St. Lawrence Seaway) = Net Debt

The growth of the national debt

Every year from 1975 to 1997 the federal government ran budgetary deficits and the debt ballooned from under $60 billion to approximately $600 billion in 1998. As Table 9.3 indicates, the debt to GDP ratio grew from 14% in 1975 to a peak in 1995 of 71%.

The case for reducing the national debt

Some people want the government to cut taxes, some want the government to spend more on health care and others want the government to pay down the national debt. Those who say the debt should be reduced use these reasons:

- Keynesian counter-cyclical fiscal policy does work if given a chance. At present the debt to GDP ratio is so high that politicians are afraid to go into more debt to counteract a decline in national income for fear that creditors will be reluctant to lend the Canadian government more money.
- Since our tax system tends to be regressive and since upper-income earners own government bonds, when we finance government spending by borrowing we redistribute wealth from low- to high-income earners.
- Foreign-held debt drains wealth out of the country and causes balance-of-payment and exchange rate problems.

- The debt is forcing future generations to pay for this generation's overspending. Borrowing to finance capital projects like bridges that future generations benefit from is acceptable, but borrowing for current consumption is not.
- Debt management can come into conflict with monetary policy. For example, if the unemployment rate is high, the Bank of Canada should lower interest rates to stimulate spending, but the Bank will not be able to lower rates because creditors may not want to hold government bonds at the lower interest rates.
- Government borrowing "crowds out" private borrowing. The government competes for loanable funds with those who also want to borrow money for things like new cars. Interest rates will tend to rise until the supply and demand for loanable funds are in balance. It could be that you are crowded out because you can't afford the higher interest costs. This will slow aggregate demand and slow the rate of economic growth.

Practice Exercise 9

1. Suppose that on a taxable income of $40,000 the tax payable is $10,000 and on a taxable income of $60,000 the tax payable is $12,000.
   (a) Is the above tax system progressive, proportional or regressive? Explain your answer.
   (b) Calculate the marginal tax rate in this case.

2. Distinguish between collective and private goods and services.

3. List four characteristics of a good tax.

4. How does a government finance its deficits?

International trade

WHY DO COUNTRIES NEED TO TRADE?

Trade makes speculation possible. Specialization is the process of breaking down large complex tasks into smaller tasks that can be repeated quickly. This process encourages automation, cuts retooling time, increases skills and takes advantage of the natural skills of individuals, groups and nations. Specialization lowers the cost of production as output increases – what economists call **economies of scale**. The end result is a rising standard of living.

For example, before Canada signed the free trade agreement with the United States, a single factory in Ontario produced a wide variety of home appliances – stoves, dishwashers, clothes dryer and refrigerators. In the space of a few months this single factory could produce enough stoves to supply the Canadian market for the whole year. So every few months the factory would halt production, retool and start producing a different appliance. With free trade, this factory now produces only refrigerators because it has access to the whole North American market. It uses the most advanced robotic technology best suited to this particular product. No time is lost to retooling, skills increase and the result is lower prices for consumers.

Absolute advantage

The gains from trade are clear in the case of **absolute advantage**. For example, assume country X and country Y have a fixed amount of land – 10 acres. Each country grows wheat on five acres and oats on the remaining five acres. We'll assume the total cost of production per acre is the same and holds constant for both products and both countries. However, output per acre differs between the two countries and so the average cost per unit of output will vary.

Before Trade	Wheat (100s of bushels)	Oats (100s of bushels)
Country X	8	4
Country Y	3	6
Total Output	11	10

Now we'll add international trade and each country will do what it does best by using all 10 acres for one crop and import the other product. Since the opportunity cost to country X of producing 100 bushels of wheat is 50 bushels of oats, X can produce another 800 bushels of wheat in exchange for giving up the production of 400 bushels of oats. Similarly country Y will be able to double its output of oats.

With Trade	Wheat (100s of bushels)	Oats (100s of bushels)
Country X	16	0
Country Y	0	12
Total Output	16	12

Notice that both countries will experience an increase in their standard of living with trade because output of both goods increases. This lowers the average cost of production per bushel. Where absolute advantage exists, specialization can improve conditions in both countries.

Comparative advantage

The principle of **comparative advantage** says that there are gains from trade even when one country can produce all goods more efficiently than other countries. Let's use the previous example but this time the products will be soya and corn (each country uses five acres for corn and five acres for soya):

Before trade	Soya (100s of bushels)	Corn (100s of bushels)
Country X	4	8
Country Y	2	1
Total Output	6	9

In this case country X is more efficient at producing both soya and corn but the *margin* of advantage differs. Country X can produce eight times as much corn as country Y with the same quantity of resources and the same total cost but only two times as much soya. Country X has a comparative advantage in the production of corn in relation to soya. Differing margins of advantage arise from differing opportunity costs. In this case a more suitable climate gives country X a comparative advantage in the production of corn. The chart indicates that the opportunity cost for country X of producing 100 more bushels of corn is 50 bushels of soya, whereas the opportunity cost for country Y of producing 100 bushels of corn is 200 bushels of soya. Country X has the lowest opportunity cost of producing corn and by the same reasoning, and country Y has the lowest opportunity cost of producing soya. For country Y the opportunity cost of producing 100 bushels of soya is 50 bushels of corn, whereas the opportunity cost to country X to produce another 100 bushels of soya is 200 bushels of corn.

Suppose we took all of country Y's land out of corn production and put it into soya production and took some of country X's land out of soya and put it into corn production, with these results:

With trade	Soya (100s of bushels)	Corn (100s of bushels)
Country X	3	10
Country Y	<u>4</u>	<u>0</u>
Total Output	<u>7</u>	<u>10</u>

The production of both soya and corn has increased for the same total cost. Therefore, average costs are lower and the standard of living in both countries will rise.

The classical theory of comparative advantage is based on the assumption that a nation's economy has resources that were hard to change and difficult to move to another country. This was true when the important factors of production were physical capital and natural resources. Today the key factors of production are **human capital** (skills, knowledge) and **entrepreneurship** (risk-taking), which are dynamic rather than static. They can move between countries and they can be improved by government policies (the quality of the schools, tax incentives). Just because an economy has a comparative advantage today doesn't mean that it will be there tomorrow.

INTERNATIONAL TRADING AGREEMENTS

Free trade agreements

NAFTA is an example of a free trade agreement. Canada and the United States created a free trade agreement in 1988 (FTA) and Mexico signed on a few years later to form the North American Free Trade Agreement. The agreement is based on the principle of **national treatment**. This principle says that a member country can establish any rules it wants, provided everyone (whether they be domestic or foreign businesses) is subject to the same treatment.

This represents the least amount of economic integration. Goods and services move without barriers among the members. Each member retains its own trade policy with respect to non-members. Customs offices remain at border crossings and a product's country of origin becomes a problem area as third-party countries try to get access to markets via the back door. For example, Japan tries to gain access to the United States through Canada because Canada's trade barriers with Japan are different from US barriers.

Common markets

There is free trade among the member nations. Not only do goods and services move freely but also the factors of production (human capital, investment capital, entrepreneurship) are allowed to move freely among members. The European Community (EC), the forerunner of the European Union (EU), is an example. Most individual countries provide one common market for all of its regions. Canada is an exception. For example, the free movement of labor among provinces is restricted by provincial legislation.

Complete economic integration

A common market controlled by a supra-national authority. The central authority not only controls trade but controls monetary, fiscal and social policies. Nation states lose a good deal of their sovereignty. Europe is adopting this model complete with its own currency – the Euro. Some people suggest that the World Trade Organization (WTO) is heading in the direction of becoming a supra-national authority.

BARRIERS TO FREE TRADE

Since WWII, barriers to free international trade have been lowered using the general principle embodied in **GATT (General Agreement on Tariffs and Trade)**. The Agreement says that if one country gives one GATT member a tariff concession, then that same concession must be extended to all other GATT members. The big prize has been to gain entry to the US domestic market. GATT has become part of the WTO which is working at reducing non-tariff barriers to trade and promoting freer trade in the service sector.

1. **Tariffs** A tariff is a tax levied on imported products. It can take the form of an ad valorem tax, which is levied on the value of the product or a specific tax, which is levied as a set amount per item. Tariffs are used to protect domestic markets from foreign competition and to raise revenue for governments. Thanks to GATT, tariff barriers have steadily

declined since WWII. In Canada's case, tariffs on some items like footwear remain high (in the 20% range), but on average tarrifs have fallen to 5%.

2.   **Quotas**   A limit is placed on the amount of imports. Voluntary export restrictions (VERs) are a form of quota where the exporter agrees to limit exports. For example, Japanese cars destined for the US market are limited by a VER agreement.

3.   **Export subsidies by government**   Lower freight rates, preferential credit terms and tax rebates within a country are examples.

4.   **Countervailing tariffs**   Countervailing tariffs are used to counteract subsidized imports in the name of "fair trade laws." The United States levies countervailing tariffs on imported steel that the United States says is being subsidized by the exporting country. Sometimes they are retained when the real reason for their existence has disappeared.

5.   **Anti-dumping duties**   Dumping refers to the practice of exporters selling a product in a foreign market for less than what the product normally sells for in the country of origin. When proven, the WTO may allow the penalized country to impose anti-dumping taxes on products from the offending country.

6.   **Foreign exchange controls**   A country deliberately keeps its foreign exchange rate undervalued. This gives its exports an unfair advantage in foreign markets and inflates the price of imports.

7.   **Trade regulations**   Complex regulations designed to keep foreign products out of domestic markets.

THE CASE FOR PROTECTIONISM
While free trade has advantages, there is a downside to be considered. Protectionism calls for a limit on free trade.

1.   **Free trade increases unemployment**   If consumers stop buying domestic products and start buying imports, domestic workers will lose their jobs. A group of organized workers who are about to lose their jobs can put pressure on a government to impose trade barriers to protect jobs.

2. **Cheap labour**   If we accept products from low wage countries, Canadian products will not be able to compete unless Canadian wage rates are reduced or there is a big increase in the productivity of Canadian workers.

3. **Strategic trade policy**   The old version of this argument was called the **infant industry argument**. It is very difficult for a new industry to get started if the industry already exists in other economies. This is particularly true where economies of scale and massive startup costs are involved. Government must provide tariff protection and subsidies until the industry is established and then it is set free to compete on the world stage. This is how the Japanese auto industry developed in the 1950s.

4. **Diversification**   If an economy specializes in industries that are prone to extreme cyclical fluctuation or if technological innovation suddenly makes an industry obsolete, the economy could suffer a great deal. Protectionism tends to diversify an economy!

5. **Free trade robs a country of its cultural and national identity (a non-economic argument)**   For instance, the US media dominates Canada's domestic marketplace. In order to reduce this influence, the Canadian government sets Canadian content rules and tries to enforce them through licensing and tax regulations. Non-economic reasons for protectionism are difficult to refute on economic grounds because they appeal to a different set of values.

Canada's Merchandise Trade by Country in billions of dollars for 1998		
	Exports	**Imports**
US	$270	$234
Japan	10	10
European Union	18	25
All Other Countries	25	34
Total	$323	$303

BALANCE OF PAYMENTS

A country's **balance of payments** accounts is a record of all monetary transactions flowing into and out of a country. It is divided into two sections, the current account and the capital account. Each item is classified either as a receipt (credit) if money is flowing into the country, or as a payment (debit) if money is flowing out.

Table 10.1
Balance of Payments Accounts for a Hypothetical Country
(measured in billions of $)

	Receipts (Credits)	Payments (Debits)	Balance
Current Account			
Trade Account			
Merchandise Exports	100		
Merchandise Imports		80	—
Visible Trade Balance			20
Service Exports	30		
Service Imports		40	—
Trade Balance			10
Capital Service Account			
Investment Income Inflow	20		
Investment Income Outflow		60	—
Current Account Balance			(30)
Capital Account			
Short-term			
Inflow	25		
Outflow		35	
Long-term Direct and Portfolio			
Inflow	80		
Outflow		30	—
Capital Account Balance			40
Basic Balance	255	245	10
Change in Official Monetary Reserves		10	
Final Balance	255	255	0

Let's explain each item:

Merchandise trade consists of visible items of trade, such as cars, newsprint and natural gas.

Trade in services includes tourism, shipping charges, insurance premiums and the wages and salaries of residents who work out of the country and non-residents who work in Canada.

The capital service account includes unilateral transfers like gifts, inheritances and immigration funds (inflow) and emigration funds (outflow). There is also interest and dividend income from invested capital. For example, a US resident who owns 100 common shares of Canadian Pacific Ltd. will receive a share of CP's profit in the form of a dividend. This item will appear as a payment on Canada's balance of payments account.

Short-term capital includes highly **liquid assets** like bank accounts and **treasury bills** (short-term government debt securities). For example, a short term capital account payment will be recorded on Canada's account when a Canadian resident opens a US dollar account at a bank in Chicago. Such accounts are very sensitive to changes in interest rates. If Canadian interest rates rise while everything else remains constant, then there will be a tendency for money to flow into Canada to take advantage of the higher investment returns.

Long-term capital is divided into two sections – portfolio and direct investments. Direct investment occurs when the purchase of assets in the other country results in gaining control of a company. For example, if Nortel buys 60% of a US-based fiber optics firm, it will appear as a direct investment item. Portfolio investments include the purchase of stocks and bonds. For example, if an American purchases 100 common shares of Canadian Pacific, it will be recorded as a portfolio receipt on Canada's balance of payment account. Even though common shares represent ownership in CP, a person would have to buy millions of them to gain control.

As indicated in Table 10.1 the balance of payments for the hypothetical country has a final balance of zero. In all cases it is zero. Each debit in Canada's account created by an import or some other transaction is matched by a credit transaction in the form of exports or financial assets moving into Canada. For example, suppose a Canadian manufacturer sells steel to a Japanese manufacturer and is paid in yen. The Canadian manufacturer will convert the yen to dollars at a Canadian bank. The bank now holds Japanese assets in the form of a yen-denominated bank account: a deposit credit in a Japanese bank which will appear as a payment on the short-term capital account section of Canada's balance-of-payments account. Thus the initial receipt for the export of steel is offset by this payment. If the bank can't find anyone to sell the yen to it can sell the yen to the Bank of Canada and this yen deposit will then appear as part of the change in the official monetary reserves on the balance-of-payments accounts. Even though the entry for the change in monetary reserves appears as a payment, it represents an increase in foreign exchange reserves held by the Bank of Canada.

When the basic balance is in a deficit position it is called unfavorable. The immediate adjustment will be made through the monetary reserve account. If this situation persists, the adjustment will come through a depreciation in the value of the currency.

Canada's merchandise trade by product type
in billions of dollars for 1998

	Exports	Imports
Machinery and equipment	$79	$101
Vehicle products	77	67
Metals, chemicals, plastic products	57	60
Agricultural products	25	17
Energy products	24	8
Forestry products	35	2
Other	26	48
Total	$323	$303

FOREIGN EXCHANGE RATES

Trade would be very difficult without a medium of exchange. At the domestic level, our Canadian dollar acts as the medium of exchange. However, if you have ever tried to buy something in Los Angeles with Canadian dollars, you know that Canadian dollars don't work very well. You must convert Canadian dollars into US dollars. The conversion price is called the exchange rate. One Canadian dollar bought $0.67 US in November 1999 or one US dollar bought $1.49 Cdn.

Let X be Canadian dollars and solve for X (ignore bank service charges).

$1 Cdn. is to $.67 US as X is to $1 US

$$\frac{1}{X} = \frac{.67}{1}$$

X = $1.49

Demand and supply theory can be used to explain how the price of one currency is determined in terms of another currency – **the foreign exchange rate**. Think of Canadian dollars as a typical product where supply and demand interact to determine the equilibrium market price. Diagram 10.1 examines exchange rate determination using Canada's balance of payments account as the starting point. Diagram 10.2 starts with the US balance of payments account.

Suppose that Canadian merchandise exports to the US increase. This would increase receipts on Canada's balance of payments account which increases the demand for Canadian dollars on foreign exchange markets. DD will shift to D_1D_1 as in Diagram 10.1 – as US importers purchase Canadian dollars. The end result is an appreciation in the value of the Canadian dollar to E_1.

For the US balance of payments account, this same event increases payments for the United States. This will increase the supply of US dollars on foreign exchange markets – SS shifts to S_1S_1 as in Diagram 10.2 – as US importers sell US dollars. The end result is a depreciation in the value of the US dollar in terms of Canadian dollar. The equilibrium rate moves from E to E_1 in Diagram 10.1 and 10.2.

Diagram 10.1   Diagram 10.2

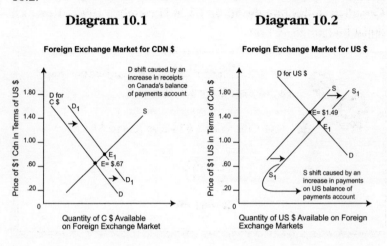

Fixed exchange rates are a combination price ceiling and price floor. As you can see in Diagram 10.3, the Bank of Canada has set $.72 US as a ceiling and $.65 US as a floor. The currency is free to float between these two benchmarks but the Bank of Canada is prepared to intervene in foreign exchange markets to prevent the dollar from rising above $.72 US or falling below $.65 US. Suppose that the supply curve for C$ shifts to S_1S_1, which drives the foreign exchange rate down below the band to E_1 (Diagram 10.3). The Bank of Canada will sell its foreign reserves and raise interest rates to increase the demand for the Canadian dollar. This action moves DD to D_1D_1 and puts the exchange rate back inside the band (E_2).

To accomplish this objective the Bank of Canada buys Canadian dollars with its foreign reserves. If it doesn't have enough foreign reserves, it borrows foreign currency. As a last resort it can borrow foreign currency from the International Monetary Fund (IMF). The Bank of Canada could increase interest rates by adopting a contractionary monetary policy that encourages an inflow of capital, causing the demand curve for the Canadian dollar to increase. On the supply side, the Bank of Canada could attempt to reduce the level of payments on Canada's balance of payments accounts, which would shift the supply curve back to its original position. For example, the federal government could raise tariffs to discourage imports and the Bank of Canada could deny residents, planning to take a holiday in the United States, the ability to purchase US dollars.

Diagram 10. 3

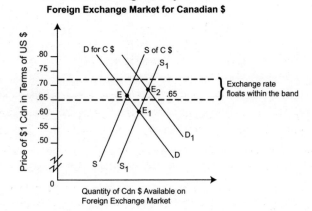

How a Fixed Exchange Rate System Works
Foreign Exchange Market for Canadian $

Why would Canada want to keep its currency deliberately undervalued?

A depreciating currency reduces the price of exports and increases the price of imports. It encourages Canadian tourists to stay at home and makes foreign travel in Canada cheaper. The net result is more economic growth and a lower Canadian unemployment rate.

However, a depreciating currency causes inflation because imports become more expensive and domestic producers face less price competition. Producers don't have to work at being efficient, they simply wait for another currency depreciation to restore their competitive edge. Although a currency depreciation provides a quick fix for economic problems, it doesn't last long. In the long run increasing productivity is what really counts if a country wants to improve its standard of living.

International monetary reserves

These reserves consist of convertible (hard) currencies like US dollars, Japanese yen and British pounds. Soft currencies like the Russian rouble are not part of the reserves because they routinely depreciate in value. The reserves also consist of gold, special drawing rights (SDRs) with the IMF and Canada's reserve position with the IMF. Official international monetary reserves are accumulated by the Bank of Canada when Canada runs basic surpluses on its balance of payments account. They are also accumulated by virtue of the fact that Canada belongs to the IMF, by the purchase of Canadian gold production and by the sale of Canada government bonds in foreign markets.

The case for a fixed exchange rate

The Mundell-Fleming model argues that **open economies** like Canada that are dependent on world trade are exposed to danger when they have floating exchange rates. For example, suppose a Canadian firm signs a contract to build airplanes for a US-based airline at a set price. After the contract is signed the Canadian dollar appreciates in value. When the Canadian firm converts US sales revenue into Canadian dollars, they will get fewer Canadian dollars. They may end up selling the planes at a loss because of the exchange rate change. Faced with this additional risk, the Canadian firm may decide not to sell outside Canada. The supporters of a fixed rate say that fiscal policy won't work for small open economies like Canada because the fiscal measures will be offset by events in other countries. Mundell argues that Canada should fix its exchange rate to the US dollar.

The case for floating exchange rates

Here are three reasons that support the existence of floating exchange rates:

- In order to defend a fixed exchange rate a central bank needs a huge pool of foreign reserves. If speculators thought that Canada's fixed exchange rate was overvalued, they would sell Canadian dollars into foreign exchange markets and the Bank of Canada would be forced to buy in order to defend the fixed rate. The Bank of Canada would run out of reserves long before speculators run out of Canadian dollars. Then the bank would have to give in and devalue the Canadian dollar. This puts Canada at the mercy of currency speculators. Mundell argues that the Bank of Canada can fight off the speculators if it uses monetary policy properly.
- A fixed exchange rate may force a country to adopt fiscal and monetary policies that conflict with domestic priorities. For example, suppose Canada has a high unemployment rate and the Bank of Canada is forced to raise interest rates to defend the fixed exchange rate. This would cause even more unemployment. Mundell argues that defending the exchange rate is a better way to promote economic stability over the long run.
- Floating rates respond daily to changes in the balance of payments so a country usually ends up with gradual changes in rates rather than the extreme changes that you get when you have a fixed rate. Mundell's response to this reason is that you never let the fixed rate of exchange change.

Managed floating exchange rates

The floating rate system currently used by Canada is called a **managed (dirty) float**. Over the long term, rates move as supply and demand conditions change but the Bank of Canada may intervene in the short run to smooth out temporary imbalances. For example, if US interest rates fell and money rushed into Canada to take advantage of our higher interest rates, the Bank of Canada would likely enter the market and buy US dollars to slow down the rate of change in the exchange rate.

Searching for an international medium of exchange

When a Canadian exporter makes a sale in Russia and the Russian importer offers to pay in Russian roubles, the Canadian exporter will likely refuse and demand payment in a hard currency. If Russia hasn't earned Canadian dollars by exporting to Canada it might have earned British pounds. Thus British pounds have facilitated trade between Canada and Russia.

Gold acted as the international medium of exchange until the 1930s when countries left the gold standard and fixed exchange rate systems in an attempt to find a solution to the Great Depression. Gold was still used but hard currencies – primarily British pounds and US dollars – were added to the list of reserves.

Today the primary international medium of exchange is the US dollar. US dollars make up the largest portion of the official reserves of central banks. The problem with this system is that world liquidity grows when the US runs basic deficits on its balance of payments account. Confidence is maintained only if the US economy prospers and there is no prospect that the US dollar will depreciate. If confidence in the US dollar falls, central banks won't want to hold US dollars as reserves and traders might not want to accept them as payment.

The International Monetary Fund (IMF) was set up after WWII in order to facilitate trade by assisting countries with balance of payments problems. The IMF issues credits called special drawing rights (SDRs) that are used by the central banks of IMF members to finance trade imbalances. In other words, SDRs are used among central banks as an international medium of exchange. However, the US dollar remains the most widely used international medium of exchange.

1. Calculate the *basic balance* on Canada's balance-of-payments
    account. Classify each item into its correct category. (All
    sums are in millions of Canadian dollars.)

    A. Canadian resident tourists spend $300 in the US.
    B. Inco, a Canadian based mining company sells nickel
        to a US-based firm for $50.
    C. Xerox of Rochester pays its Canadian resident
        shareholders a dividend of $20.
    D. Non-residents buy a Toronto company for $650.
    E. The Quebec government pays its non-resident
        bondholders interest of $100.
    F. Canadian residents buy US government T-bills for $200.
    G. The Canadian government pays troops stationed in
        Europe $150.
    H. Non-residents purchase common shares in Newbridge
        on the TSE for $60.

2. If Canada adopts a contractionary monetary interest rates in
    Canada will _____ (fall/rise). This change in interest rates
    will cause money to flow into _____ (United States/Canada)
    and in turn cause the Canadian dollar to _____
    (appreciate/depreciate). As a result Canadian merchandise
    exports will become ____ (less/more) expensive in the
    United States.

APPENDIX ONE

Answers to practice exercises

Practice Exercise 1

1. (a) normative economics   (b) ceteris parabus
   (c) microeconomics   (d) consumer is king
   (e) hypothesis   (f) capital
   (g) rational thinking

2. (a) 20 consumer goods   (b) 5 capital goods
   (c) 9 consumer goods   (d) 4 consumer goods
   (e) 2 capital goods

Practice Exercise 2

1. (i) increase   (ii) increase
   (iii) decrease   (iv) increase
   (v) no change   (vi) increase

2. As the price increased so did TR making the demand curve price inelastic. $E_d = 0.33$

3. $E_d = \dfrac{\% \text{ change in } Q_d}{\% \text{ change in price}}$

   Let X = % change in Q_d

   $1.2 = \dfrac{X}{.20}$

   X = .24   Therefore as a result of the import tax, Q_d decreases by 24%. Widgets are price elastic in this price range.

Practice exercise 3

1. (a) 2.00×4 million bushels $= \$8$ million
   (b) 2 million bushels;   4.5 million bushels
   (c) 2.5 million bushels; 2.5 million $\times \$3.00 = \$7.5$ million
   (d) 3.00×4.5 million $= \$13.5$ million ;
       13.5 million — $\$ 8$ million $= \$5.5$ million

Practice exercise 4

1. To maximize profits this firm should produce 8 or 9 units because at this output MR = MC = \$30.
2. TR ($\$30 \times 8$ units) — TC at 8 units = profit of \$75
3. Break even occurs at a price of \$20 because this is where ATC is at a minimum.
4. Shut down occurs at a price of \$2 because this is where AVC is at a minimum.

Practice exercise 5

GNE = $45 + 21 + 30 + 12 - 15 = 93$
NI = $3 + 17 + 6 + 52 = 78$
GDP = NI $(78) + 2 + 13$
    GDP measured by the income approach = 93

Practice exercise 6

1. (a) prices have decreased   (b) transportation
   (c) $\dfrac{127 - 119.9}{119.9}$ X 100 $= 5.9\%$
2. \$40 million $\div$ .05 $=$ \$800 million

3.

Year	NI	Required Stock of Capital	Net (New) Investment
1	30	240	240
2	40	320	80
3	42	336	16

3. (a) 8   (b) falls from 80 to 16

4. The difference between actual NI and intended AE causes the cycle. If actual NI is greater than intended AE, NI will face downward pressure.

Practice exercise 7

1. Canadian Tire "money" isn't widely accepted as a medium of exchange.

2. Change in M = $\frac{1}{.07}$ × ($50,000 — (.07 X $50,000)

   = $\frac{1}{.07}$ × $46,500

   = $ 664,286

3. high; fall; down; buyer; increase; more

Practice exercise 8

1.

Actual National Income

2. fiscal policy -> budgetary surpluses,
   contractionary monetary policy

3. time lags;
   conflicts with social and political objectives;
   disruptive international capital flows

Practice exercise 9

1. (a) Regressive – at the $40,000 income level the tax rate is
      25% (10/40) whereas at the $60,000 income level
      the tax rate is 20% (12/60)
   (b) The marginal tax rate is 10%. (Δ taxes/Δ income.
      In this case $(2 \div 20 \times 100)$

2. Collective goods and services benefit the community as a
   whole (for example, national defense) whereas the benefits of
   private goods and services go to specific individuals (for
   example, clothes).
   As a result collective goods tend to be provided by government
   and paid for from general taxation whereas private good are
   provided by the market and are paid for by users fees.

3. convenient; hard to evade; equitable (iv) tax incidence is clear

4. the sale of government bonds and/or printing more money

Practice exercise 10

	Receipts	Payments	Balance
Current Account			
Trade			
A		300	
B	50		
G		150	
Capital Service			
C	20		
E		100	___
Current Account Balance			(480)
Capital Account			
Short Term			
F		200	
Long Term			
D	650		
H	60		___
Capital Account Balance			510
Basic Balance	780	750	30

2. rise; Canada; appreciate; more

Model final examination

(100 marks, 2.5 hours)

Tips to students writing economics examinations:

- Use the marks allotted to the question as a guide to determine how much time you should spend answering each question. For example, the essay question on this examination has a value of 40 marks out of a total of 100 marks. If you are given 2.5 hours to write the exam you should spend approximately 40% of the time (60 minutes) answering this essay question. If you knew all the material, you could spend two hours on the essay question but that would leave you too little time for the rest of the exam. Consequently you can't say everything and the teacher knows this. Organize the answer to the essay question in point form before you write and focus on the key concepts covered in the course.

- Remember that an essay question should show the depth and breadth of your knowledge.

- To get an A you will have to show that you understand current economic issues by using real examples. To build up your general knowledge, read about current economic issues on a regular basis.

- Bring a calculator with you to the exam.

- Many of the multiple choice questions and short answer questions require that you do some calculations or analysis. Don't guess – do the calculations! For example, to answer multiple choice question 6, sketch a supply-demand diagram in the margin and then analyze the question using the diagram.

- Those who have not taken an economics course could answer the essay question. They could talk about all those lazy people who just don't want to work. But this approach will not get you an A. What the teacher wants to see is your ability to apply economic terms, principles and theories to a specific issue.
- How you write something is as important as the factual content. If your sentence structure is weak, your spelling is poor, your answer is not organized, you will not get an A.

Part A (multiple choice, 20 marks)

1. The production-possibilities curve can be used to illustrate the concept of:
   (a) comparative and absolute advantage
   (b) elasticity of demand
   (c) diminishing marginal utility
   (d) opportunity costs

2. How goods are produced in a command type of economic system is determined by:
   (a) consumer spending patterns
   (b) government officials
   (c) the method that generates the most profit
   (d) the method that will cause the least amount of environmental damage

3. The price of product X increased from $1.50 to $2.00 per unit and the quantity demanded decreased from 45 to 25 units. The price-elasticity coefficient of demand for product X in this price range is:
   (a) 0.5   (b) 1.0   (c) 2.0   (d) 2.5

4. If the demand for product X increases as the price of product Y decreases, we can be fairly certain that:
   (a) product X and product Y are substitutes
   (b) product Y is price elastic and product X is price inelastic
   (c) X and Y are inferior products
   (d) X and Y are complementary products

5. An increase in demand for product Y and a decrease in supply of product Y will:
   (a) increase market price and increase the quantity sold
   (b) increase market price while the quantity sold remains the same
   (c) increase market price and decrease quantity sold
   (d) increase market price and affect quantity sold in an indeterminate way

6. If supply increases, ceteris paribus, then there will be:
   (a) an increase in price and a decrease in quantity
   (b) an increase in price and an increase in quantity
   (c) a decrease in price and an increase in quantity
   (d) a decrease in price and a decrease in quantity

7. In which of the following situations is a firm maximizing its profits, or minimizing its losses?
   (a) MR > MC and TR > TC   (b) MR < MC and TR < TC
   (c) MR = MC and TR < TVC   (d) MR = MC and TR > TVC

8. Given that nominal GDP is $834 billion and the GDP deflator is 106.6, then real GDP is:
   (a) $889 billion   (b) $782.4 billion
   (c) $ 728.6 billion   (d) $ 940.6 billion

9. In 1999 a fruit farmer sells strawberries to a food processor for $ 1000. The processor turns the strawberries into frozen packages of berries and sells them to a wholesaler for $3200. At the end of 1999 the strawberries are part of the wholesaler's inventory. In the year 2000 the strawberries are sold by retailers for $4800. What amount will statisticians add to GDP for the year 2000 as a result of the above activities?
   (a) $1600   (b) $4800
   (c) $600   (d) zero since the strawberries were produced in 1999

10. According to the multiplier principle, if the MPS = .20 and there is a $12 billion decline in investment spending, then NI, ceteris paribus, would fall by:
    (a) $24 billion   (b) $1.67 billion
    (c) $60 billion   (d) $12 billion

11. According to the accelerator principle, if the capital-output ratio (accelerator) is 3:1 and there is an increase in consumer spending of $9 billion, then investment spending, ceteris paribus, would increase by:
    (a) $3 billion   (b) $27 billion
    (c) $33.3 billion   (d) $12 billion

12. The process of creating deposit money by banks is possible because
    (a) bank loan losses are very small
    (b) of the fractional reserve system
    (c) modern economies have a fiat money system
    (d) money is a good standard of value

13. If a bank currently holds $500 million in deposits and $60 million in reserves and has a target reserve ratio of 4%, this bank has:
    (a) excess reserves of $40 million
    (b) excess reserves of $20 million
    (c) excess reserves of $24 million
    (d) excess reserves of $60 million

14. Unemployment caused by automated teller machines (ATMs) can best be described as:
    (a) structural unemployment
    (b) frictional unemployment
    (c) seasonal unemployment
    (d) cyclical unemployment

15. The most effective way to moderate the business cycle is counter-cyclical fiscal policy according to:
    (a) monetarist economists
    (b) classical economists
    (c) Keynesian economists
    (d) supply-side economists

16. Income distribution patterns can best be illustrated using the:
    (a) Phillips curve
    (b) Laffer curve
    (c) production-possibilities curve
    (d) Lorenz curve

17. Canada's payroll taxes (for example, EI) are generally regarded as an example of :
    (a) regressive taxes
    (b) proportional taxes
    (c) ability to pay taxes
    (d) progressive taxes

18. Gains from trade are created by international specialization when:
    (a) absolute and comparative advantages exist among countries
    (b) economies of scale occur
    (c) countries have different opportunity costs
    (d) all of the above

19. The infant industry argument is an old version of the _____ reason for defending protectionism:
    (a) diversification
    (b) strategic trade policy
    (c) cheap labor
    (d) unemployment

20. If 1 Japanese yen will buy $.005 Cdn then $1 Cdn will buy:
    (a) 200 yen   (b) 150 yen   (c) 100 yen   (d) 50 yen

Part B (short answer, 40 marks)

1. For each of the following statements, indicate whether it refers to the market or the command type of economic system and indicate which economic question the statement answers.

    (a) Goals set by planners determine how resources will be used.
    (b) The consumer is king.
    (c) Many goods are made available free of charge.
    (d) Goods are distributed according to a person's ability to pay.
    (e) Competition and the profit motive drive the production process.
    (f) A central authority decides whether to produce butter or margarine.

    Answer this question in the space provided below.

Economic System	Economic Decision			
	What	How	For	Whom
Market	_____	_____	_____	_____
Command	_____	_____	_____	_____

2. Consider the effects that each of the following events has on the market for beef. In the space provided draw the supply or the demand curve that best represents each situation. In addition indicate whether there will be an increase (+), decrease (−) or no change (0) in demand, supply, equilibrium price and quantity exchanged.

	Demand	Supply	Equilibrium Price	Quantity Exchanged
(a) A good that is a substitute for beef increases in price.	_____	_____	_____	_____
(b) A widespread drought increases the cost of cattle feed.	_____	_____	_____	_____
(c) A good that is complementary to beef increases in price.	_____	_____	_____	_____

3. Identify the economic term most closely associated with each description.
   (a) profit maximization point _____
   (b) time period when all costs become variable _____
   (c) AVC = MC _____
   (d) when profit more than covers explicit and implicit costs

   _____

   (e) the result when all MC curves are added together

   _____

   (f) increasing returns in the long run _____
   (g) ATC = MC _____
   (h) kinked-demand curve _____
   (i) the cause of a fall in MP _____
   (j) the extra cost incurred to produce an additional unit of output _____

4. A perfectly competitive firm is in the following position:
   Output   6000 units   Total fixed costs $3000
   Market price $2.00 per unit Total variable costs $6000
   Marginal cost $1.75
   (a) Calculate ATC at this output level.

   _____

   (b) Calculate profit per unit at this output level. _____

(c) Calculate total profit at this output level. _____

(d) Explain why this firm is not maximizing profits._____

(e) Should this firm produce more or less in order to maximize profits? _____

5. Indicate, by writing GNE, NI or N beside each item, whether it is included in GNE, NI or neither (N) of these accounts.

_____ (a) the government pays for new road construction

_____ (b) tips received by a waiter

_____ (c) sale of Canadian nickel to a Japanese-based automaker

_____ (d) employment insurance benefits received by unemployed Canadians

_____ (e) purchase of a new truck

_____ (f) salary received by a used furniture salesman

6. Match the description in Column B with the term in Column A that it is most closely associated with.

Column A		Column B
_____ recessionary gap	(a)	short-term fluctuations in GDP
_____ business cycle	(b)	when the price level falls
_____ structural	(c)	unemployment caused by a change in AE
_____ frictional		
_____ deflation	(d)	amount that investment changes from an initial change in consumer spending
_____ cyclical		
_____ multiplier		
_____ accelerator	(e)	potential GDP > actual GDP
_____ inflationary gap	(f)	potential GDP < actual GDP
_____ MPS	(g)	the amount of each extra dollar of income saved
	(h)	unemployment caused by a change in technology
	(i)	the amount NI changes from a change in spending
	(j)	unemployment caused by labor mobility

7. One unit of factor inputs can produce varying amounts of gadgets and widgets.

	Gadgets	Widgets
Country A	9	3
Country B	3	2

(a) The chart is an example of the law of _____ advantage.

(b) The opportunity cost to A of producing one widget is _____ gadgets.

(c) The opportunity cost to B of producing one widget is _____ gadgets.

(d) Therefore, B has a comparative advantage in the production of _____ .

8. On the supply-demand diagrams, indicate by drawing a supply or demand curve the effect that each event would have on the foreign exchange rate.

(a) an increase in dividend payments by Canadian-based firms to non-resident shareholders in the United States

(b) a decrease in Canadian tourism to the United States

(c) Ontario Hydro sells a debenture in the United States and transfers the money to Canada

127

Part C (essay, 40 marks)

Answer the following three-part question in sentence and paragraph form. Ten (10) marks will be assigned for organization, grammar and spelling. Since each part of the question is interrelated, read all three parts before you start to write. Each part will be evaluated using the following criteria:

- shows cause and effect relationship
- uses economic principles and theories
- uses relevant and diverse examples
- uses diagrams and makes connections between what is written and diagrams

Unemployment was the most pressing economic issue facing Canada in the past decade. Throughout the 1990s Canada's unemployment rate remained stubbornly high. It was approximately double the US unemployment rate. Youth unemployment (15-24 years of age) was approximately 15%.

Part I –   Examine two important causes of unemployment in Canada (10 marks).

Part II –   Propose two policies that would reduce the unemployment rate (10 marks).

Part III – Evaluate the two policies you proposed in Part II in terms of the impact that they would have on other areas of the economy (10 marks).

Answers to model final exam

Part A (multiple choice, 20 marks)

1. (d)	2. (b)	3. (c)	4. (d)	5. (d)
6. (c)	7. (d)	8. (b)	9. (a)	10. (c)
11. (b)	12. (b)	13. (a)	14. (a)	15. (c)
16. (d)	17. (a)	18. (d)	19. (b)	20. (a)

Part B (short answer, 40 marks)

1.

	What	How	For Whom
Market	(b)	(e)	(d)
Command	(f)	(a)	(c)

2.

		D	S	EP	QE
(a)		+	0	+	+
(b)		0	—	+	—
(c)		—	0	—	—

3. (a) MR = MC   (b) long run   (c) shut down
   (d) economic profits   (e) market supply curve
   (f) economies of scale   (g) break even   (h) oligopoly
   (i) diminishing returns   (j) MC

4.   (a) $9000 / $6000 = $1.50   (b) $2.00 — $1.50 = $.50
      (c) $.50 × 6000 = $3000   (d) MR > MC
      (e) produce more

5.   (a) GNE   (b) NI   (c) GNE   (d) N   (e) GNE   (f) NI

6.   e, a, h, j, b, c, i, d, f, g

7.   (a) comparative   7. (b) 3   7. (c) 1.5   7. (d) widgets

8.   (a)   (b)   (c)

ANSWER TO ESSAY QUESTION

Part 1 – Two causes

Cyclical and structural unemployment were the two primary causes of unemployment in Canada in the 1990s. Cyclical unemployment is triggered by a decline in aggregate spending. As spending falls, workers are laid off and the more workers who are laid off, the more spending falls. Once the cyclical downturn starts, it is hard to stop and the economy ends up in a recession as it heads into the trough of a business cycle. The decline in aggregate spending can be caused by a decrease in any of the components of GNE – G (government), I (investment), C (consumption), X – M (net exports).

Typically, investment spending is singled out as the primary cause of cyclical unemployment because it is the most volatile component of GNE. For example, if consumer spending is the same this year as last year, investment spending will decline according to the accelerator principle. The accelerator and the multiplier principles acting together can result in a dramatic decline in aggregate expenditures (AE).

The accompanying diagram uses a 45° line to show the equality between spending and income. Actual spending (GNE) is always equal to the national income (NI). The problem arises when the actual level of NI isn't high enough to provide full employment (Y_f), as indicated on the recessionary gap diagram.

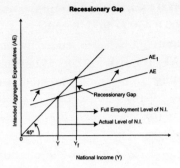

Recessionary Gap

Structural unemployment is the second primary cause of unemployment. Whereas cyclical unemployment focuses on the demand side of the market, structural unemployment looks at the supply side of the market. If it costs more to produce in Canada than in the United States or in some other part of the world, then firms will invest elsewhere. For example, taxes in Canada are higher than in the United States and taxes are just another cost of doing business. High taxes drive jobs out of Canada.

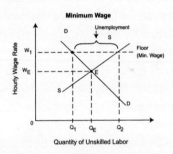

Minimum Wage

Government regulations add to the cost of production. For example, the minimum wage law sets a price floor below which wages can't fall. This creates unemployment, as illustrated in the accompanying diagram. Unemployment is represented by the horizontal distance between Q_1 and Q_2 on the minimum wage diagram. As indicated in the question, youth unemployment was very high and the minimum wage law helps to keep it high. The mismatch between the skills that firms want and the skills that workers possess is another example of structural unemployment. Rapidly changing technology and a reluctance on the part of workers to adjust is making this a problem area.

Part 2 – Two policies to reduce unemployment

The aim of these policy proposals is not to reduce unemployment to zero but rather to reduce the unemployment rate to what economists call the natural rate of unemployment (NAIRU). There will always be some unemployment such as frictional unemployment caused by workers who are in the process of moving from one job to another.

Keynesian counter-cyclical fiscal and monetary policies, as the title indicates, take aim at cyclical unemployment. Classical economists thought that the market system, if left alone, would return to the full-employment level of income but the experience of the Great Depression convinced Keynes and policymakers that the economy could get stuck with chronic unemployment. Keynesian economics attempts to increase aggregate expenditure from AE to AE_1 as indicated in the recessionary gap diagram where the full-employment level of NI is located. Keynesians would do this by adopting expansionary fiscal and monetary policies. On the fiscal side, government spending should be increased and taxes should be decreased with a resulting budgetary deficit for the government. On the monetary side, the money supply should be expanded at a rate in excess of the potential growth in GDP. The Bank of Canada would be a net buyer of bonds in the open market through open market operations. This would increase the reserves of the chartered banks, interest rates would fall and more loans would be made. The end result is an increase in AE.

Supply-side economists look for solutions on the supply side of the market. There must be more incentives for producers: cutting taxes, deregulating industries, ending the welfare mentality and generally providing an environment in which firms can get on with the business of becoming more productive. For example, supply-siders would get rid of the minimum wage law. By removing the minimum wage, the hourly wage rate would fall from W_I to W_E (refer to the minimum wage diagram) but job opportunities would grow from Q_I to Q_E. Productivity, that is output per unit of input and the cost of the inputs (for example, labor costs), is the key to providing job opportunities.

Part 3 – Evaluation of the two policy proposals

In the early years of the 1990s, Canada was in a cyclical downturn and the Keynesian model seemed appropriate. Unfortunately, Canada was stuck in a fiscal trap. In good economic times and bad economic times, Canada ran budgetary deficits, so by the early 1990s Canada had a huge national debt. The government was reluctant to budget for even bigger deficits for fear that foreign investors, who are big holders of Government of Canada bonds, would lose confidence in Canada and refuse to buy more bonds. Worse, they might sell the bonds they already owned. This would have put severe downward pressure on the Canadian dollar which was already trading at a historical low of $.63 US. The government couldn't take the risk, so Keynesian fiscal and monetary measures were not used.

Fortunately the US economy came to the rescue. NAFTA and booming US domestic market boosted Canada's exports to the US. Exports not government spending kick-started the economy and AE moved higher. Supply-siders say the only thing that orthodox Keynesian fiscal policy produces is inflation and they point to the Phillips curve as proof. Giving consumers more money to spend isn't going to improve employment if productivity is the problem.

Under the Reagan presidency in the United States in the 1980s, supply-side economics was tried. Top income tax rates were cut from 70% to 30% and industries like the airlines were deregulated. The US economy limped along in the 1980s and because of the huge tax cuts the US national debt ballooned into the trillions of dollars. In the 1990s the US economy took off, the US unemployment rate was close to or at the NAIRU and supply-siders liked to take the credit.

In Canada the federal and provincial governments were beginning to adopt more of the supply-siders', ideas. Results included less government spending on education, health care, welfare and roads and higher users fees (for example, tuition). The critics including the Keynesians, argued that such policies increase income inequality (for example, lowering minimum wages) and ruin the infrastructure (for example, roads), which are essential prerequisites to a healthy economy. Keynesians argue that the supply-siders have got it backwards. Production and supply improve when there is a demand for the production. Firms won't invest when demand is weak. Supply doesn't generate its own demand.

**For fifty years, Coles Notes have been helping
students get through high school and university.
New Coles Notes will help get you through the rest of life.**

Look for these NEW COLES NOTES!

LIFESTYLE

- Wine
- Bartending
- Beer
- Wedding
- Opera
- Casino Gambling
- Better Bridge
- Better Chess
- Better Tennis
- Better Golf
- Public Speaking
- Speed Reading
- Cooking 101
- Scholarships and Bursaries
- Cats and Cat Care
- Dogs and Dog Care

PARENTING

- Your Child: The First Year
- Your Child: The Terrific Twos
- Your Child: Ages Three and Four
- Your Child: Age Five to Eight
- Your Child: Age Nine to Twelve
- Your Child: The Teenage Years
- Raising A Reader
- Helping Your Child in Math

SPORTS FOR KIDS

- Basketball for Kids
- Baseball for Kids
- Hockey for Kids
- Soccer for Kids
- Gymnastics for Kids
- Martial Arts for Kids

BUSINESS

- Effective Business Presentations
- Accounting for Small Business
- Write Effective Business Letters
- Write a Great Résumé
- Do A Great Job Interview
- Start Your Own Small Business
- Get Ahead at Work

PERSONAL FINANCE

- Basic Investing
- Investing in Stocks
- Investing in Mutual Funds
- Buying and Selling Your Home
- Plan Your Estate
- Develop a Personal Financial Plan

PHRASE BOOKS

- French
- Spanish
- Italian
- German
- Russian
- Japanese
- Greek

GARDENING

- Indoor Gardening
- Perennial Gardening
- Herb Gardening
- Organic Gardening

MEDICAL SERIES

- Prostate Cancer
- Breast Cancer
- Thyroid Problems

**Coles Notes and New Coles Notes are available at the following stores:
Chapters • Coles *• World's Biggest Bookstore**